AQA

REVISE AQA GCSE

English and English Language

REVISION GUIDE

Higher

Series Consultant: Harry Smith

Author: David Grant

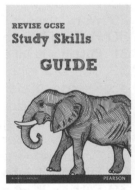

Contents

1-to-1 page match with the Revision Workbook
ISBN 9781447940708

SECTION A: READING

SECTION B: WRITING

A small bit of small print
AQA publishes Sample Assessment Material and the Specification on its website. This is the official content and this book should be used in conjunction with it. The questions in ***Now try this*** have been written to help you practise every topic in the book. Remember: the real exam questions may not look like this.

NO

Questions 1 and 2

Before you get stuck into your revision for Section A: Reading, you need to know –

- **what sort of questions you will be answering**
- how long you will have to spend on each answer
- how to pick out the key information in the question.

In Section A, you will have to read **three** unseen source texts and answer **four** questions. This page covers Questions 1 and 2. Don't try to answer the exam questions on this page – just get used to the style.

Question 1 tests your ability to **retrieve information and ideas** from the first text, **Source 1**.

This means picking out relevant pieces of information that answer the question.

It tests the following assessment objective:

> Read and understand texts, selecting material appropriate to purpose, collating from different sources and making comparisons and cross-references as appropriate.

This is the opening of an example of Source 1.

Source 1

Supermarkets are killing us

Shetland's dairy farmers say their farms are facing an uncertain future as

This is an example of Question 1.

1 What do you learn from **Source 1** about the problems facing dairy farmers in the Shetland Islands? *(8 marks)*

Question 2 tests your ability to **understand and interpret presentational features** (e.g. headlines and images) in the second text, **Source 2**.

This means commenting closely on how the text is presented and its effect on the reader.

It tests the following assessment objective:

> Explain and evaluate how writers use linguistic, grammatical, structural and presentational features to achieve effects and engage and influence the reader, supporting your comments with detailed textual references.

This is the opening of an example of Source 2.

Source 2

Food of the future

Growing population and dwindling resources may mean a major re-think of what we are prepared to eat

This is an example of Question 2.

2 Explain how the headline, subheading and image are effective and how they link with the text. *(8 marks)*

Now try this

Answer the following questions in three or four words using the information on this page.

1 What skill will Question 1 of your exam test you on?

2 What skill will Question 2 of your exam test you on?

Had a look ☐ Nearly there ☐ Nailed it! ☐

Questions 3 and 4

Before you get stuck into your revision for Section A: Reading, you need to know –

- **what sort of questions you will be answering**
- how long you will have to spend on each answer
- how to pick out the key information in the question.

In Section A, you will have to read **three** unseen source texts and answer **four** questions. This page covers Questions 3 and 4. Don't try to answer the exam questions on this page – just get used to the style.

Question 3 tests your ability to **understand and interpret meaning** in the third text, **Source 3**.

This means identifying and inferring, and explaining information relevant to the question.

It tests the following assessment objective:

Read and understand texts, selecting material appropriate to purpose, collating from different sources and making comparisons and cross-references as appropriate.

This is an example of Question 3.

This is the opening of an example of Source 3.

Source 3

Confessions of a stuntman

One of the most dangerous and hair-raising escapades of my career came when I was asked to

3 Explain some of the writer's thoughts and feelings as he prepares to jump from the helicopter. *(8 marks)*

Question 4 tests your ability to **compare the effectiveness of language** in two of the texts.

This means identifying, comparing, and contrasting language features, and commenting closely on their effect.

It tests both of the assessment objectives at once.

Explain and evaluate how writers use linguistic, grammatical, structural and presentational features to achieve effects and engage and influence the reader, supporting your comments with detailed textual references.

This is an example of Question 4.

4 Compare the ways in which language is used for effect in the two texts. Give some examples and analyse what the effects are. *(16 marks)*

When answering this question you will need to refer to **Source 3**, and **either Source 1** or **Source 2**. You will compare two of the texts, one of which you have chosen.

Now try this

Answer the following questions in four or five words using the information on this page.

1. What skill will Question 3 of your exam test you on?
2. What is the difference between the skills which Question 3 will test you on and the skills which Question 1 will test you on?
3. What skill will Question 4 of your exam test you on?

Planning your exam time

Before you get stuck into your revision for Section A: Reading, you need to know –

- what sort of questions you will be answering
- **how long you will have to spend on each answer**
- how to pick out the key information in the question.

Running out of time is one of the most common ways that students lose marks in their exam. You should plan your time to get the most out of every minute. This page will help you prepare for this.

The English / English Language Unit 1 exam is 2 hours and 15 minutes long.

Section A: Reading is worth 40 marks.

Section B: Writing is worth 40 marks.

You should spend:

- 15 minutes reading the source texts and questions for Section A: Reading
- 1 hour answering the questions in Section A: Reading
- 1 hour answering the questions in Section B: Writing.

Also see page 53

The first 15 minutes

You should spend the first 15 minutes of the exam reading the source texts and the questions you will be asked about them. So when you are told that you may start, you could:

1. **Read the questions** to find out what you're looking for when you read the source texts.
2. **Skim read the source texts** to get a rough idea of what they are about and the main ideas.
3. **Read the source texts carefully,** thinking about the information, ideas, and presentational and language features that you will write about.
4. **Read Question 1 again, then go through Source 1,** highlighting information and ideas that will help you answer the question.
5. **Do the same for Question 2** and **Source 2**, then **Question 3** and **Source 3**.
6. **Decide which two texts you will write about in Question 4,** then go through them highlighting relevant features. We will cover annotating the sources in more detail on page 7.

Worked example

Work out how long to spend on Question 1 in **Section A: Reading**.

The Section A part of the exam should take 1 hour, or 60 minutes, and is worth 40 marks. That gives me 1½ minutes for every mark. So if Question 1 is worth 8 marks, I should spend 12 minutes answering it.

Now try this

Work out how long you need to spend on Questions 2 *(8 marks)*, 3 *(8 marks)* and 4 *(16 marks)*, in minutes.

To check your answer, add all the times for all four questions together – they should add up to 60 (minutes).

Had a look ☐ Nearly there ☐ Nailed it! ☐

Reading the questions

Before you get stuck into your revision for Section A: Reading, you need to know –

- what sort of questions you will be answering
- how long you will have to spend on each answer
- **how to pick out the key information in the question.**

You need to read each question on the exam paper very carefully to make sure you know exactly what it is asking you to do. This page will help you practise how to focus on the key words in questions. Don't try to answer the exam questions on this page – focus on picking out the key words.

1 What do you learn from **Source 1** about the problems facing dairy farmers in the Shetland Islands? *(8 marks)*

Check which source you are being asked to write about.

Check the focus of the question – that is, the information and ideas you are being asked to write about.

2 Explain how the headline and picture are effective and how they link with the text. *(8 marks)*

Pick out the key words in the question. Make sure you focus only on these features.

You must describe these features and **explain** how they are **effective**.

Make sure you comment on how these features link to the content of the text.

3 Explain some of the writer's thoughts and feelings as he prepares to jump from the helicopter. *(8 marks)*

Don't just describe them. You are being asked to **explain** them.

Check if you should write about the whole text or just one specific part of it.

Make sure you know what the question is asking you to focus on – and make sure you don't write about anything else.

Now try this

Now you need to refer to **Source 3**, and either **Source 1** or **Source 2**. You are going to compare the **two** texts, one of which you have chosen.

4 Compare the different ways in which language is used for effect in the **two** texts. Give some examples and analyse what the effects are. *(16 marks)*

Look at the exam-style question opposite.

- Which source texts should you write about?
- What are the key words in the question that tell you what to do?
- What feature of the texts is this question asking you to write about?
- What does the question advise you to do when writing your answer?
- How many marks is this question worth?
- How long should you spend writing your answer to this question?

Approaching the exam paper

Once you're in the exam hall, you need to get to work as soon as you turn over the exam paper. This page will show you how to put what you've learned over the last four pages into practice. Don't try to answer the exam questions on this page – focus on picking out key information and working out how long you can spend on each question.

For each question make sure you identify **exactly** what the examiner is asking you to do. Look at how this student has underlined key features of Question 1:

✓ Identifies key focus of question.

✓ Highlights two areas to look for in the text.

Section A: Reading

Answer **all** questions in this section.

You are advised to spend about one hour on this section.

1 What do you learn from **Source 1** about Barry Barnes' early life and how it has affected his health? *(8 marks)*

✓ Identifies which source text to write about.

Now read **Source 2**.

2 Explain how the headline and picture are effective and how they link to the text. *(8 marks)*

Timing plan

Reading the question and source texts (9.00–9.15am)

Q1: 12 mins (9.15–9.27am)

Q2: 12 mins (9.27–9.39am)

This student has made a timing plan. Their exam started at 9am, so they have noted down rough start and end times for each question, including leaving 15 minutes to read the question and source texts.

Now read **Source 3**.

3 Explain some of the thoughts and feelings Sally Bland has during her South American expedition. *(8 marks)*

Now you need to refer to **Source 3** and either **Source 1** or **Source 2**. You are going to compare the **two texts**, one of which you have chosen.

4 Compare the different ways in which language is used for effect in the **two texts**. Give some examples and analyse the effects. *(16 marks)*

Now try this

1 Look at the timing plan above. Complete the plan for Questions 3 and 4.

2 Look at the way that the key information has been picked out of Question 1. Now pick out the key features of Questions 2, 3 and 4.

Make sure you identify:
- which source to write about
- the key focus of the question
- what you are being asked to write about.

Had a look ☐ Nearly there ☐ Nailed it! ☐

Skimming for the main idea

Time is precious in the exam so it's a good idea to skim-read the source text before reading it in detail. This will give you a good idea of what the text is about.

Key features

Look at these key places when you skim-read a text.

The heading.

The first sentence of each paragraph.

The last sentence of the text.

Britain's 'litter epidemic' costs almost £1bn every year

A Keep Britain Tidy survey shows the cost of employing litter pickers and buying equipment to clear chewing gum rose by £100 million in the last year.

The Local Government Association said it was 'environmental vandalism' that is robbing councils of money to pay for schools and hospitals.

The chief executive of Keep Britain Tidy said, 'it is quite obscene that we, as a nation, have to spend more than £¾ billion clearing up the rubbish that people can't be bothered to put in a bin'.

Summing up

Think about how you would sum up the entire article in one sentence. Here are two possibilities for the article on the right:

- Britain wastes a lot of money on tidying up litter.
- Litter is expensive.

Now try this

Look at this newspaper article for 20 seconds. How could you sum it up in one sentence?

Make sure that you look at:

- the headline
- the first sentence of each paragraph
- the last sentence of the article.

High-school prom washout: we're just too British

School's nearly out for summer, and we all know what that means: prom time. Nowadays it seems every limo company/helicopter hiring racket in the country is contending with a jammed phone line as hundreds of 16- to 18-year-olds try to reserve that much sought-after 'grand entrance'.

The average prom costs parents £209. I find it rather sad that the prom is morphing from what it should be – a party with your mates – to what it really shouldn't – a chance to show off how much cash your mum and dad have.

I blame My Super Sweet 16 and American teen movies for making our sixth formers think that they need transport and an entourage worthy of J-Lo in order to have a good time at a party.

Annotating the sources

Get used to highlighting, underlining or circling parts of a source that you can use to support your answers.

Highlight and annotate

Look at this question.

> **3** Explain some of the writer's thoughts and feelings about weightlifting and weightlifters. *(8 marks)*

You can gather information for your answer by annotating the source like this:

Feels frightened / sharing their pain – emotive language.

Emphasises pain and fear.

Suggests admiration?

Sounds dangerous but spectacular – simile.

Don't just highlight useful quotes.
Note down:

- the effect on the reader
- the technique used to achieve it.

Source 1

'I used to hate weightlifting but I've grown to love it'

The noise is terrifying. Eeeeyaaaahah. Crash. Aaaaaaaaaaaaaaeugh! Thud. Close your eyes and you could be in a war zone. Open them, and it doesn't get much better. A man with a tiny belted waist and pumped muscles twists his face into an agonising gurn, lifts the bar above his head, and lets it fall. The weights explode on to the floor like fireworks.

Now try this

Read the next paragraph of the newspaper article opposite. Quickly highlight and annotate any words or phrases from this text that you could use to answer this exam-style question:

> **4** Compare the different ways in which language is used for effect in the **two** texts. Give some examples and analyse what the effects are. *(16 marks)*

Here in the gym at Leeds Metropolitan University, British weightlifters are training for the Olympics. They are an extraordinarily dedicated bunch of athletes. They have to be. The British team have given up their jobs or studies to survive on £100 a week from UK Sport, there are no cash prizes for winning, and few sponsorship deals. Training is torture, their hands are callused and blistered, and they know they have next to no chance of winning medals. But that's not the point.

Had a look ☐ Nearly there ☐ Nailed it! ☐

Selecting information

Section A, Question 1 tests your ability to **retrieve** information and ideas from a source text. You need to pick out and use **only the information that is relevant** to the question.

Look at the question below:

> **1** What do you learn from **Source 1** about Suzanne Collins? *(8 marks)*

To answer it you need to pick out relevant information about Collins herself. Look at these examples.

These tell you about Collins herself.

These tell you about her book and the film of her book.

Note that the question asks about the author, so this information is not relevant.

Source 1

Suzanne Collins: Hunger Games author

There are many bestselling children's authors but only rarely do any break through into the universal cultural consciousness. Now along comes Suzanne Collins, a 49-year-old from Connecticut, in the USA, with The Hunger Games trilogy.

It's too early to know how durable this series will prove, but the signs so far are good. It has spent more than 100 weeks on the New York Times bestseller list. The film has made converts of even the most curmudgeonly critics, grossing more than \$531m (£327m) worldwide in its first four weeks. More than 1m copies of the books are now in print in the UK, and last month Amazon announced that Collins had become the bestselling Kindle author so far.

Now try this

Read the next paragraph of the article about Suzanne Collins.

What do you learn about her in this paragraph? Select relevant information.

Remember to:
- select information that will help you answer the question
- ignore information that will not.

The woman behind the phenomenon is a bit of a mystery. She is married to a TV actor, but she doesn't do publicity, and hasn't even met her UK publishers. Is her reluctance to self-publicise innocent or knowing? Either way, it's striking in the context of The Hunger Games, which is set in a nation, Panem, in which everything is televised. A fragmented post-apocalyptic society is ruled by the fascistic Capitol, which keeps the masses quiet by feeding them reality war games featuring teenagers who must fight to the last one standing.

Purpose and audience

The first things you should think about when you read a text are its purpose and its audience.

Purpose

The purpose of a text is the reason why it was written. Texts can do any of these things:

- describe
- explain
- inform
- advise
- argue
- persuade
- review
- analyse

Audience

The audience of a text is who the text is aimed at. A writer might aim their text at an audience:

- of men, or women or both
- from a specific age group or age range
- with specific interests.

Worked example

1 What do you learn from **Source 1** about the holiday in Turkey? *(8 marks)*

The text gives lots of information about several activities and facilities suitable for young families. It would appeal to them because it is 'hassle-free', so parents can relax while their children enjoy themselves. Activities for young children include playing around the pool and going on a gentle boat trip. The hotel is near the harbour so it's not too far for small children to walk.

Here you will see that this student has recognised:

- the **purpose** of the text is to **inform**
- the **audience** is **parents with young families**.

This has helped her to pick out relevant information to use in her answer.

Source 1

A tour for toddlers

Exodus's Turkey Toddler Adventure has been designed with young families in mind. It's a hassle-free mix of relaxing and exploring, based in a harbour town in southern Turkey. Activities include a gentle boat ride to an island, snorkelling over a sunken city, and castle and farm visits. The hotel, which is 10 minutes' walk from the harbour, has a good restaurant and an excellent pool area.

EXAM SKILL

Recognising the **purpose** and **audience** of a text will help you comment on how and why the following things are effective:

- the writer's choice of information
- the use of presentation and language.

Use this skill to help you improve the quality of your writing.

Now try this

Show your awareness of purpose and audience as you answer this exam-style question.

1 What do you learn from **Source 2** about the tour of the Hebrides? *(8 marks)*

Remember to think about:

- the purpose of the text
- its audience.

Source 2

A Grand Tour of the Hebrides

Our grand tour takes in all the beauty and diversity of this very special environment. Two comfortable hotels ensure that this holiday is as relaxing as possible while offering great variety and a true journey of discovery which will live long in the memory.

Putting it into practice

In Section A, Question 1 of your exam, you will need to retrieve information and ideas from a text. Read **Source 1**, then look at the question on the next page.

Source 1

Two hours' homework a night linked to better school results

Spending more than two hours a night doing homework is linked to achieving better results in English, maths and science, according to a major study which has tracked the progress of 3,000 children over the past 15 years.

Spending any time doing homework showed benefits, but the effects were greater for students who put in two to three hours a night, according to the study published by the Department for Education.

The finding on homework runs counter to previous research which shows a 'relatively modest' link between homework and achievement at secondary school.

The academics involved in the latest research say their study emphasises what students actually do, rather than how much work the school has set.

Pam Sammons, a Professor of Education at Oxford University, said that time spent on homework reflected the influence of the school – whether students were expected to do homework – as well as students' enjoyment of their subjects.

Sammons said: 'That's one of the reasons Indian and Chinese students do better. They tend to put more time in. It's to do with your effort as well as your ability.

'What we're not saying is that everyone should do large amounts, but if we could shift some of those who spend no time or half an hour into [doing] one to two hours – one of the reasons private schools' results are better is that there's more expectation of homework.'

The research also finds that students who reported that they enjoyed school got better results. 'This is in contrast to findings during primary school where "enjoyment of school" was not related to academic attainment,' researchers said.

Schools could ensure children had a better experience by improving the 'behavioural climate', making schoolwork interesting and making children feel supported by teachers, Sammons said.

'Children who did well from disadvantaged backgrounds were backed by parents who valued learning and encouraged extra-curricular activities. 'Parents' own resilience in the face of hardship provided a role model for their children's efforts,' the research says.

The study underlines the importance of a good primary school. Children who attended an 'academically effective' primary school did better at maths and science in later life. The study did not find a link with performance in English.

Ministers have scrapped guidelines setting out how much homework children should be set amid criticism that it can interfere with family life. Scrapping the guidelines frees head teachers to set their own homework policy, the government says.

Putting it into practice

Look at this exam-style question and read the extracts from two sample student answers.

Worked example

1 Read **Source 1**. What do you learn from the article about factors which can affect students' results at school? *(8 marks)*

Sample answer

Looking carefully at **Source 1**, I have learned that homework really helps improve students' results. Some people did a survey of lots of children for several years which showed that doing more homework had greater benefits for students. This runs counter to previous research which shows only a modest link between homework and achievement at school.

✓ Begins with a summary of the main point.

✗ More detail needed here.

You should avoid using chunks of text that are not entirely relevant to the question.

Improved sample answer

According to a recent survey, homework can significantly improve students' results. Although doing any homework can help students' achievement, the survey found that students who did two or three hours homework a night benefited the most. The researchers point out that the school's expectations are a significant factor in the amount of time students give to homework. This suggests that the school's expectations can have a major influence on students' achievement.

✓ Clearly states the key focus of the text, and gives an effective summary of the survey's main finding.

✓ A significant deduction from the information given in the source.

This answer is clearly focused on what the question asks. Always check that you do the same.

Retrieving information and ideas

For a question like this you should:

- spend about 10–15 minutes on your answer
- skim read the source first to get the main ideas
- read the source carefully and highlight **relevant information**
- check that the information you have highlighted is relevant.

Now try this

Complete the 'Improved sample answer'. Aim to identify at least **three** more relevant points.

Remember to:

- select only information relevant to the task
- include relevant detail.

Remember also that you should not copy out chunks of text.

Had a look ☐ Nearly there ☐ Nailed it! ☐

The writer's viewpoint

If you can identify a writer's viewpoint, you will be able to understand their ideas and comment on how the writer has expressed them.

Viewpoint

A **viewpoint** is the writer's attitude and opinion on a particular subject.

- Most texts reveal something about the writer's viewpoint.
- But in some texts the writer gives the facts as clearly as possible without revealing their own viewpoint. These texts are **unbiased**.

Identifying the writer's viewpoint

1 Decide whether the viewpoint is positive or negative.

2 Look closely at these things to develop your understanding.

- **The heading:** suggests the writer thinks the beauty industry is covering up a horrible truth.
- **The writer's choice of ideas:** opening paragraph focuses on the difference between consumers' 'assumption' and 'the truth'.
- **The writer's choice of language:** immediate focus on 'animal suffering'.

Source 1

Animal testing is the beauty industry's well-kept ugly secret

Many consumers still shop under the assumption that cosmetics animal suffering is a thing of the past. The truth, however, is altogether harder to swallow: thousands of animals are still used to test cosmetic chemicals.

Now try this

Read the next paragraph of the article. How does it tell you more about the writer's point of view?

Write **one** or **two** sentences commenting on the writer's:

- choice of ideas
- use of language.

Many companies continue to test on animals in countries such as the United States of America, China and Brazil. In these countries, animals continue to have cosmetic chemicals forced down their throats, dripped into their eyes and applied to their shaved skin, sometimes in doses high enough to kill.

Fact, opinion and expert evidence

Writers make their ideas more persuasive or convincing by supporting them with facts, opinions and expert evidence.

fact
Something that can be **proved** to be true.
Example: *'Manchester is a city in the United Kingdom.'*

opinion
An idea or viewpoint that the writer or speaker **believes** to be true.
Example: *'Manchester is the greatest city on earth.'*

expert evidence
Facts or opinions provided by an expert on the subject
Example: *'Barry Chesham, a travel writer with over 30 years' experience, says: 'Manchester is the greatest city on earth.'*

Improving your exam answer

Referring to how the writer has used facts, opinions and expert evidence can improve your answers.

Read **Source 1**. In this article, the writer has:

- made his viewpoint very clear by opening with **a strong opinion**
- supported his opinion with **a fact** – a statistic used as evidence to prove his point
- referred to **expert evidence** to support his point even more.

Source 1

Gang culture turning kids to lives of crime

A severe epidemic in Britain's inner cities has seen boys as young as eight are being coerced to join older street thugs

A 10.6 per cent increase in serious youth violence in the six months to last October has been linked to gangs. The Metropolitan Police's new anti-gang squad recently arrested 315 suspected gang members.

According to Scotland Yard, there are 250 gangs in London, each with several hundred members.

In Croydon, Surrey, one of the flashpoints of last summer's riots, I meet 13-year-old James.

'Three older boys said I should join their gang,' James remembers. 'They wanted me to look after things for them so they wouldn't get caught.'

'I was really afraid. I didn't think I would get away. I was surrounded, and I was followed a few times after that.'

He was lucky. David Mitchell, who runs the Gang Avoidance Project in Nottingham, says many school-age gang recruits are made to look after drugs and weapons with no firm promise of being accepted.

However, once they are involved, the financial rewards can be huge. 'They believe there is nothing else out there,' says Mr Mitchell. 'Some can easily make £4,000 a week.'

Now try this

Read **Source 1**. Note down **one** further fact, **one** further opinion and **one** further piece of expert evidence that the writer uses to support his viewpoint.

Make sure you know the difference between a fact, an opinion, and expert evidence.

Had a look ☐ Nearly there ☐ Nailed it! ☐

Inference

A writer does not always state their meaning **explicitly**. Sometimes you have to work out what the writer is suggesting or **implying**. This is called making an **inference**.

Reading between the lines

When you read an extract, you can infer information about the **feelings**, **thoughts**, **attitudes** and **actions** of the writer and the people they are writing about.

In this newspaper article, the writer has chosen words or phrases carefully to **suggest** or **imply** certain things.

Source 1

Six days to get up... 90 seconds to get down

Russian climber and BASE jumper Valery Rozov recently added another highlight to his incredible career in extreme sports by setting a new world record with a jump from the top of Shivling, a 6543m mountain in the Indian part of the Himalayas.

Suggests a major achievement.

Suggests the writer's positive attitude to this achievement.

Implies this is an extraordinary feat.

Implies the extreme scale and danger of Rozov's jump.

Worked example

3 Read the extract above. Explain some of the writer's thoughts and feelings about Rozov's jump. *(8 marks)*

The writer is clearly impressed by Rozov's achievement, describing his career as 'incredible' and this jump as a 'highlight' suggesting it is one of his most extraordinary feats. The writer emphasises this by pointing out the height of the mountain and that Rozov set a new world record, implying the scale and danger of the jump.

Using one-word quotations allows you to focus on the inferences made by the writer.

A fully developed answer should:

- refer to evidence from the extract
- comment on what can be inferred from the evidence
- develop the point with further comments or additional evidence from the source.

Now try this

Read the next paragraph of the newspaper article and answer the exam-style question below.

3 Explain some of the writer's thoughts and feelings about Rozov's jump. *(8 marks)*

Remember to choose quotations of just one or two words to support your answer, and comment on what each word implies.

The 47-year-old Russian's breathtaking feats, such as jumping into the active volcano Kamtschatka and from Ulvetanna Peak in the Antarctic, have made him famous the world over.

Thanks to his exceptional climbing skills, Rozov recently took things to the next level by completing the most challenging BASE jump ever performed.

Point-Evidence-Explain

P-E-E is a technique you can use in your answers to make them clearer and better organised.

- First, you make your **point**.
- Then you provide **evidence** to support it.
- Finally you should **explain** what the evidence tells us.

In Section A, Questions 2, 3 and 4, you will be asked to **explain** or **compare** features of source texts. To do this effectively, you need to **support** your ideas with **evidence** from the text, and **explain** its **effect**.

P-E-E in practice

You should use a range of connecting phrases to link your point, evidence and explanation.

1 Make your point: The writer uses | The article focuses on

2 Introduce your evidence: For example, | The writer describes | For instance,

3 Introduce your explanation: This gives the impression that | The writer is implying that | This suggests | This shows

Worked example

Read **Source 1** opposite. Write about the different ways in which language is used for effect.

The writer uses a lot of emotive language to draw attention to the problems faced by dairy farmers. For example, she describes the supermarkets 'crippling' farmers by reducing the price they are paid for milk. This gives the impression that the supermarkets are acting like bullies, physically hurting the farmers.

Source 1

The cut in supermarket milk prices is crippling dairy farmers, who are now planning to take part in demonstrations to make their feelings known. They say that the price cut is causing major financial problems for farmers and their employees.

The paragraph opens with a clear **point**, focusing on the use of language in the article.

The point is supported with **evidence**: a short quotation from the article.

The evidence is **explained** with a comment on the choice of language.

Now try this

1 Read the extract opposite. Choose a short quotation to support the following point:

The writer uses a stream of negative language to describe Britain.

2 Now write a sentence commenting on the writer's choice of language.

Remember to use connecting phrases to link your **point**, **evidence** and **explanation**.

Switzerland: the sort of country Britain should try to be

Compared to sleazy, crime-ridden Britain, with its stagnant economy, soaring unemployment, decaying social services, mushrooming debts and uncontrolled state spending – not to mention its useless, clueless and incompetent political leadership – Switzerland is still what Britain once was: an island of the blessed, a patch of prosperity in a continent sliding into a black hole.

Had a look ☐ Nearly there ☐ Nailed it! ☐

Putting it into practice

In Section A, Question 1 of your exam, you will need to locate and retrieve information and ideas from a text. Read **Source 1** then look at the question on the next page.

Source 1

Scott Mills: my Saturday job

The Radio 1 DJ explains how volunteering, passion and persistence led to his dream career

I was 12 when I started working at a local hospital radio station in Southampton, near where I grew up. I'd always wanted to do radio from as far back as I can remember. Actually, I think I got the job because my nan rang them up! I spent two years volunteering – on a Tuesday evening and all day on Saturday.

Initially I just helped out behind the scenes – in the newsroom, making tea, being the general dogsbody. I was nervous because I was quite shy. I wasn't the best at meeting new people, but I got better at it and grew in confidence.

Some people there were more welcoming than others, but despite my age I think it was clear that I really wanted to do this as a career. The committee were all in their 60s and a bit old-school. They had been doing the hospital radio in the same way forever; I think some of them are still there now. When a 12-year-old comes along and is very keen they are a bit ... oh, who is this? Eventually they chucked me out for being too young.

There was a younger crowd in on Sundays, who were in their 20s and who I could relate to. So I went in on Sundays and they let me do loads: operating equipment and going on air. The first thing I would do on air was the chart rundown, which I prepared lovingly every week.

I remember when my friend Lee, who I'm still in contact with, sat me down one day and said: 'Right, let's see how good you are.' So we did an off-air radio show where I operated all of the equipment. I remember being the most excited I've ever been. But eventually the older people sent me a letter saying I couldn't operate the

equipment because I was too young – they basically told me not to come in any more. I think it was something to do with not being insured. I was gutted. I used to love it.

I never thought I'd make it as a presenter because I wasn't confident enough. I was planning on working behind the scenes, not as a presenter. This was the first time I realised I could do it. Before that, it was just a dream.

I'm from a small town in Hampshire; I had a dream of what I wanted to do and I followed it through. If I hadn't hung out with those hospital radio people on a voluntary basis, I wouldn't have had the skills to get my first job.

Putting it into practice

Look at the exam-style question below and read the extracts from two students' answers.

Worked example

1 Read **Source 1**. What do you learn from Scott Mills' article about the Radio 1 DJ's early life? *(8 marks)*

Retrieving information and ideas

For a question like this you should:

- spend about 10–15 minutes
- skim-read the source first to get the main ideas
- read the source carefully and highlight **relevant information**
- check that the information you have highlighted is relevant.

Sample answer

Scott Mills was 12 when he started working in a local hospital radio station in Southampton. He spent two years working there as a volunteer until he was 'chucked out' because he was too young.

He was shy when he was young so he thought he would end up working in radio behind the scenes, and not be a presenter, although he dreamed of it and loved it when he tried it. Hospital radio was where he got the skills to get his first job.

✓ An effective introduction, though it is copied from the text.

✗ Although this synthesises information from different parts of the text it does not fully focus on Mills himself.

Note that these two points summarise information from the text but do not fully explore the issues raised or make connections between them.

Improved sample answer

Scott Mills was only twelve when he volunteered to work in hospital radio which shows how determined and ambitious he was even from a young age. But he was also shy – he only got the job because his nan phoned them up which emphasises how unconfident he was as a child.

This lack of confidence also shows when he describes himself as being 'nervous' even though he was working as a dogsbody, making tea.

✓ Selects key information and comments perceptively.

✓ Connects further relevant information from across the text, supporting and developing the previous point.

Now try this

Complete the 'Improved sample answer', aiming to identify at least **three** more relevant points.

Remember to:

- select and connect information from the whole text
- avoid copying or paraphrasing relevant information.

Had a look ☐ Nearly there ☐ Nailed it! ☐

Identifying presentational devices 1

Presentational devices affect how a text looks, either on screen or on paper. You will be asked about these in Section A, Question 2.

Colour

Colour is a significant presentational feature. It reflects mood and can even suggest your response. For example:

- black: evil, death, formality
- red: passion, fire, blood, danger
- orange: energy, warmth, happiness
- yellow: happiness, sunshine, cowardice
- green: nature, environment, jealousy
- blue: calm, cleanliness, sky, water
- purple: luxury, wealth, nobility
- white: purity, peace, winter

Plan ahead

Do

- Have your own revision timetable – start planning well before exams begin. Your teacher should be able to help.
- Make your books, notes and essays user-friendly. Use headings, highlighting and revision cards, and get tips on other revision techniques from teachers and friends with experience of exams. You could also consider buying revision guides.
- Take notes of the important points when revising. Try to answer the questions of past exam papers – explain answers to tricky questions to someone else.
- Everyone revises differently. Find out what routine suits you best - alone or with a friend or parent/carer; early morning or late at night; short, sharp bursts or longer sessions; with music or without noise.
- Ask for help from your teacher/learning mentor, parent/carer or a friend if there are things you don't understand.

Don't

- Don't leave revision to the last minute.
- Don't avoid revising subjects you don't like or find difficult.
- Don't forget that there is life beyond revision and exams.
- Don't cram ALL night before an exam.

Pamper yourself

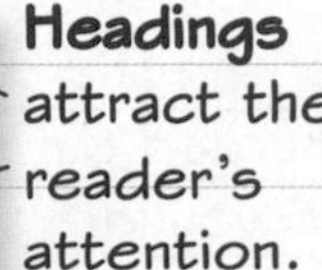

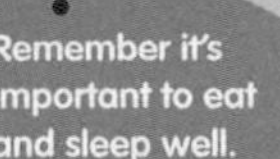

Remember it's important to eat and sleep well.

Put yourself first – this is an important time for you. Try to talk to your family about how they can make studying a little easier for you – for example, by agreeing times when you can have your own space, when they will try to be a little quieter around the house and when you'd rather not be disturbed (except perhaps for the occasional treat, such as a drink or snack).

Don't revise all the time

Make sure you give yourself time each day to relax, taking breaks to do something you enjoy – watch TV, listen to music, read a book or go out for a walk.

Headings attract the reader's attention.

Subheadings guide and direct the reader's understanding.

Images reflect meaning and influence the reader's response.

Font choice can help to emphasise certain points and can suggest a tone to the reader.

Remember:

- **font format** (using bold, italics or colour) can affect meaning and emphasise a point
- **images** can be drawings, photographs or other types of graphics
- **capital letters** make things stand out.

Now try this

Choose **three** presentational features of the leaflet extract above. Write **one** or **two** sentences about the effect of each one.

Identifying presentational devices 2

Presentational and structural devices are used to organise the text. You will be asked about these in Section A, Question 2.

Sections and boxes can be used to:

- highlight key information
- organise different sections of information.

Sections and boxes can be used to make a text more accessible. Look out for information in bordered boxes or on blocks of coloured background.

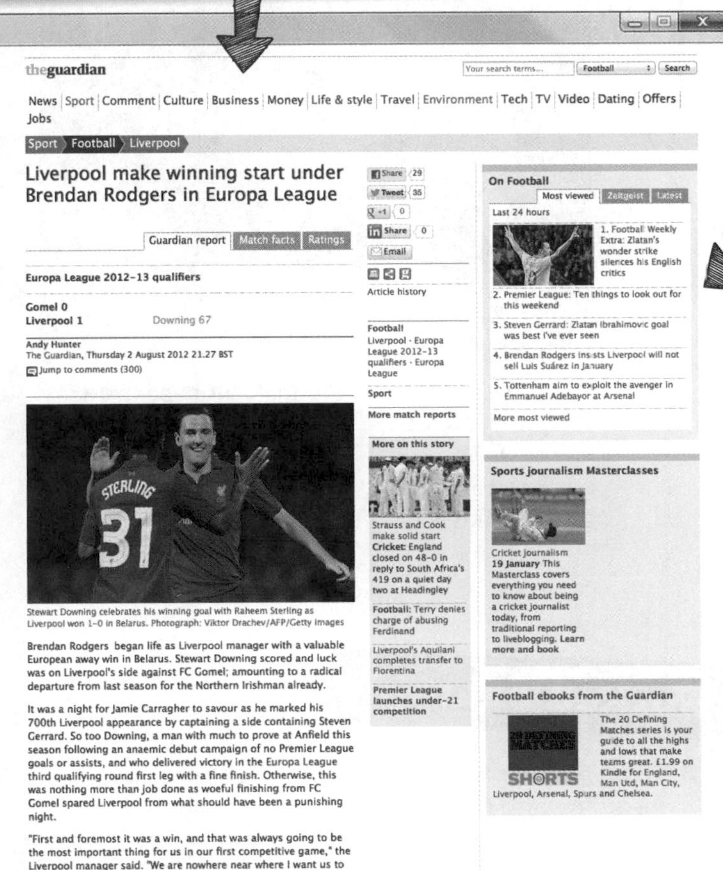

theguardian

Your search terms... | Football | Search

News | Sport | Comment | Culture | Business | Money | Life & style | Travel | Environment | Tech | TV | Video | Dating | Offers | Jobs

Sport › Football › Liverpool

Liverpool make winning start under Brendan Rodgers in Europa League

Share 29 | Tweet 35 | +1 0 | Share 0 | Email

Article history

Guardian report | Match facts | Ratings

Europa League 2012–13 qualifiers

Gomel 0
Liverpool 1 Downing 67

Andy Hunter
The Guardian, Thursday 2 August 2012 21.27 BST
Jump to comments (300)

Stewart Downing celebrates his winning goal with Raheem Sterling as Liverpool won 1–0 in Belarus. Photograph: Viktor Drachev/AFP/Getty Images

Brendan Rodgers began life as Liverpool manager with a valuable European away win in Belarus. Stewart Downing scored and luck was on Liverpool's side against FC Gomel; amounting to a radical departure from last season for the Northern Irishman already.

It was a night for Jamie Carragher to savour as he marked his 700th Liverpool appearance by captaining a side containing Steven Gerrard. So too Downing, a man with much to prove at Anfield this season following an anaemic debut campaign of no Premier League goals or assists, and who delivered victory in the Europa League third qualifying round first leg with a fine finish. Otherwise, this was nothing more than job done as woeful finishing from FC Gomel spared Liverpool from what should have been a punishing night.

"First and foremost it was a win, and that was always going to be the most important thing for us in our first competitive game," the Liverpool manager said. "We are nowhere near where I want us to be at the moment in relation to fluency and charisma within the team. But what is important until we arrive at that time – and we have plenty of work still to do – is that we fight for the shirt, defend and play with desire and passion. We definitely did that."

Football
Liverpool · Europa League 2012–13 qualifiers · Europa League

Sport

More match reports

More on this story

Strauss and Cook make solid start
Cricket: England closed on 48–0 in reply to South Africa's 419 on a quiet day two at Headingley

Football: Terry denies charge of abusing Ferdinand

Liverpool's Aquilani completes transfer to Florentina

Premier League launches under-21 competition

On Football

Most viewed | Zeitgeist | Latest

Last 24 hours

1. Football Weekly Extra: Zlatan's wonder strike silences his English critics
2. Premier League: Ten things to look out for this weekend
3. Steven Gerrard: Zlatan Ibrahimovic goal was best I've ever seen
4. Brendan Rodgers insists Liverpool will not sell Luis Suárez in January
5. Tottenham aim to exploit the avenger in Emmanuel Adebayor at Arsenal

More most viewed

Sports journalism Masterclasses

Cricket journalism
19 January This Masterclass covers everything you need to know about being a cricket journalist today, from traditional reporting to liveblogging. **Learn more and book**

Football ebooks from the Guardian

SHORTS

The 20 Defining Matches series is your guide to all the highs and lows that make teams great. £1.99 on Kindle for England, Man Utd, Man City, Liverpool, Arsenal, Spurs and Chelsea.

Bullet points and numbering make information quick and easy to digest. They can add visual variety to a text, and reduce the number of words. Remember that numbered lists can also be used to sequence or rank information.

Tables can be used for large amounts of information, making it easier to read and understand.

Paragraphs break up blocks of text by organising them into sections. Note that short paragraphs can make a text easier and quicker to read, and create a sense of pace.

Now try this

Choose a leaflet (one that has come through your letterbox, for example) or a webpage. Identify the presentational and structural features it uses to organise information and make it more accessible to the reader. Write **one** or **two** sentences about each structural feature.

Had a look ☐ Nearly there ☐ Nailed it! ☐

Using P-E-E to comment on presentational devices

In Section A, Question 2, you will explore the effect of a text's presentational and / or structural features. Point-evidence-explain will help you to organise your answers.

Answering questions

For Section A, Question 2, you will need to **explain** the effect of presentational features such as headlines, subheads and photographs. For example, you could explain how effectively the photograph in **Source 1** links with the text.

Headlines can grab attention.

Subheadings can lead the reader further into text.

Photographs can support both text and headlines.

Source 1

A little competition

It's not a dangerous thing – school sports days can help nurture ambition in children

I am writing this having just returned from my daughter's sports day – at which, incidentally, she won the 100 metre sprint. You will have gathered from this that her school operates a pretty traditional kind of event.

You can use Point-Evidence-Explain to comment on presentational and structural devices.

Worked example

2 Read **Source 1**. Explain how the headline, sub-headline and photograph are effective and how they link with the text. *(8 marks)*

The bold headline grabs the reader's attention but does not give them much information. It hints at the content of the article, by referring to the issue of 'competition' at primary school sports days, perhaps intriguing the reader. It also uses a pun on the word 'little' as a school sports day is a competition for little people. The pun creates a humorous tone reflecting the humorous tone of the article.

A clear point about the headline.

Evidence and comment on its effect on the reader.

A second piece of evidence and a comment linking the headline to the text.

Now try this

Look again at **Source 1**. Write another Point-Evidence-Explain paragraph in which you explain how **either** the headline or the subheading **or** the picture are effective comment on how they link with the text.

Commenting on headlines

When you write about headlines and subheadings, you should focus closely on their specific effects.

Headlines are big and bold

They grab the reader's attention, making them want to read on ...

HOWEVER, these comments are rather obvious. There's a lot more you can say about headlines to improve your response.

Does the **headline** intrigue the reader by not stating exactly what the story is about?

You should think about information it gives **and** the information it withholds.

Has the writer used alliteration or repetition to emphasise a key point or create impact?

Has a **subheading** been used to add more information and intrigue?

You can develop your explanations by thinking more about a headline's language features.

Has the writer used a rhetorical question to entice the reader to read on to discover the answer?

For example, a pun could create a humorous tone, or emotive language could add to the drama.

Has the writer used language that reflects the tone of the article?

Worked example

Read **Source 1**. What are the effects of the headline?

The headline clearly states what the article is about. It emphasises the key point that the jump was made 'without a parachute' to surprise and astonish the reader, adding the statistic that the jump was made from a height of '2,400 feet' to add to the effect.

Remember, you can:

- use more than one quotation to make your point
- point out more than one effect.

A general point about the headline.

A short quotation.

A detailed comment focusing on effect.

Source 1

Stuntman completes 2,400ft skydive without a parachute

Now try this

Look at **Source 2** opposite. Write a P-E-E paragraph about the headline and subheading, focusing on their effect.

Remember that P-E-E stands for Point-Evidence-Explain.

Source 2

Storm batters Birmingham

Seven families left homeless as torrential rain and 100mph winds strike city

Had a look ☐ Nearly there ☐ Nailed it! ☐

Image and effect

Images do more than illustrate a text. They can influence your response to it, too. When you write about images, think carefully about the effect they have on the reader.

Image and impact

The **effect** of an image can sometimes be stronger than the text itself. The photograph on this website has been carefully chosen to **persuade** readers to give money to an animal charity.

This is what Benjie looked like when he was brought into our rescue centre. Your donations could save other dogs like Benjie. Please give generously.

Donate now

Illustrating or undermining

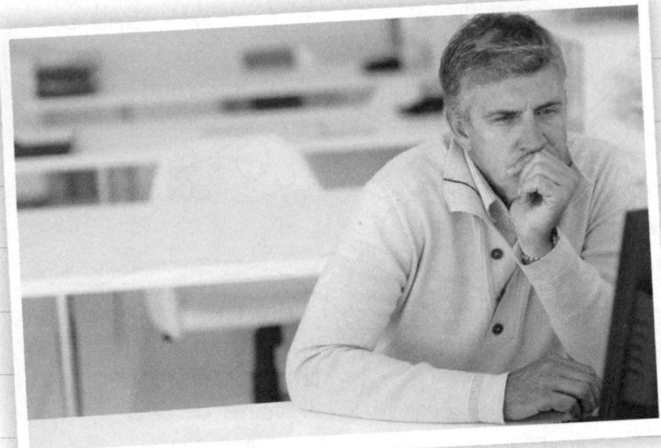

Images can alter the way a reader responds to a text. For example, this photograph illustrates a local politician's concern in headline 1. But in headline 2, the impact on the reader could be to question whether the image or the text tells the truth.

Local MP 'deeply concerned' about education report

Local MP agrees economic recovery is 'on target'

Backdrop and camera angle

Camera settings and angles can also be used to create an **effect**. In this image:

- The building has been photographed from a low angle. This makes it seem taller and more imposing.
- The dark sky adds to the atmosphere of gloom and threat.

Now try this

Write a description of the photo you would like to accompany an article you have written entitled:

The holiday of a lifetime!

Remember to include:

- what the photo will show
- whether it will have people in it (what they will be doing and how they look)
- what the weather will be like.

Linking comments on presentation to the text

To improve your response on Section A, Question 2, you need to comment on how **presentation** supports the **content** of a text.

Content and presentation

Presentational and structural features can help the text:

- **appeal** to its audience
- **achieve** its purpose
- **reinforce** its viewpoint.

Your comments should focus on how the presentational and structural features do this.

EXAM SKILL

When you are writing about presentation,
Do comment on:

- specific language
- how each feature affects the reader
- how the effect is created.

Do not:

- simply describe presentational features
- make obvious comments such as 'the headline is big and bold, and grabs the reader's attention'.

Use this skill to help you improve the quality of your writing.

Source 1

The world is closer to a food crisis than most people realise

Unless we move quickly to adopt new population, energy, and water policies, the goal of eradicating hunger will remain just that

Food riots in Algeria in 2008.

In the early spring this year, US farmers were on their way to planting some 96m acres in corn, the most in 75 years. A warm early spring got the crop off to a great start. Analysts were predicting the largest corn harvest on record. As spring turned into summer, the thermometer began to rise.

The headline:

- uses emotive language to emphasise the problem
- draws attention to the central issue
- highlights the scale of the problem
- accentuates the relevance of the issue to the reader.

The subheading:

- summarises the writer's viewpoint
- explains the problem and the writer's solution
- uses a list to draw attention to the scale of the problem.

The image and caption:

- reflect the crisis which the article warns about
- make clear the worrying consequences of recent food shortages.

Now try this

Write **two** or **three** paragraphs explaining how the headline, subheading and photograph in **Source 1** are effective and how they link with the text.

Had a look ☐ Nearly there ☐ Nailed it! ☐

Selecting evidence

It is important to always support your answers with carefully chosen, relevant evidence from the text.

Relevant evidence

The evidence you choose must support your points **and** allow you to comment closely on the writer's choices. To do this, you should choose evidence that:

- allows you to focus on answering the question
- contains a word, phrase or sentence structure you think the writer has used for effect.

Worked example

1 Read **Source 1**. Explain some of the writer's thoughts and feelings about free running. *(8 marks)*

Source 1

Free runners hit the streets as urban craze sweeps Britain

It is one of the hottest days of the summer and outside London's South Bank Centre Jake Penny (15) and his friend, Joe Scandrett (13), are hurling themselves around a warren of concrete pedestrian underpasses. Using ledges, metal handrails and anything else within reach, the two teenagers cause passers-by to gape by executing back-flips and somersaults high into the air, each time landing gracefully and silently on the pavement. What is the appeal of this peculiar sport in the urban jungle?

Sample answer

The writer thinks that free running is a strange sport. He describes it as 'peculiar'. This suggests he does not like it very much.

This student has picked out and written about the only word that directly states the writer's feelings about free running.

Remember that the more examples you give, the more opportunity you have to comment on the writer's choice of language.

Improved sample answer

'hurling themselves' suggests danger, recklessness, action ...

'gape' suggests spectators and writer are amazed and impressed ...

'gracefully and silently' suggests impressed with their skill ...

'What is the appeal of this peculiar sport in the urban jungle?' is a rhetorical question that suggests the writer doesn't understand its appeal ...

These quotations provide many more opportunities to comment effectively and produce a better answer.

Now try this

Write **two** or **three** P-E-E paragraphs answering the exam-style question above.

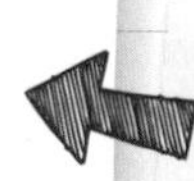

Remember to choose evidence that will let you to comment on the writer's **choices** and their **effect**. You can use the examples given, or choose some of your own.

Embedding quotations

You can use long quotes or short quotes as evidence.

Longer quotations

When you use a longer quotation you should give it some space.

Sample answer

The writer uses a rhetorical question to sum up the key point in her article:

'Why do some people feel they can say things on a social networking website which they would not dare to say to someone's face?'

This question engages the reader, making them consider this key point, and also suggests that she is horrified and mystified by the way people behave on the internet.

Longer quotes: what to do

1. Introduce your longer quotation with a colon.
2. Start the quotation on a new line.
3. Put your quotation in quotation marks.
4. Copy your quotation accurately.
5. Start your explanation on a new line.

Shorter quotations

When you use shorter quotations you should aim to embed them in your paragraph.

Sample answer

The writer condemns some users of social networking websites as 'cruel' and 'offensive' although she does confess that she has become 'obsessed' with them. This strong choice of positive and negative language suggests that she has mixed feelings about these sites.

Short quotes: what to do

Remember these things.

1. You do not need to introduce each quotation with a colon or start a new line.
2. Put each quotation in quotation marks.
3. Make sure the sentence containing the embedded quotations makes sense.
4. Choose single-word quotations very carefully to ensure you can make an effective comment on them.

The effect of short quotes

Shorter quotations are often more effective than longer ones.

- They show that you can identify key words and phrases in the text.
- They allow you to focus on the writer's specific language choices.
- You don't waste time and ink copying out large chunks of the source text.

Source 1

Why sport matters

Stars at the Olympics, like those at Wimbledon, can **inspire** young people to develop their own talents and build their own **self-respect**, whether they are brilliant or just run-of-the-mill at the games they learn to love. Team sports help bind people and communities together. **Sport brings young people out of themselves, away from computer and television screens**. It makes them **healthy** and **motivated**.

Now try this

Write **two** P-E-E paragraphs about the writer's thoughts and feelings about sport in **Source 1**, using the bold quotations.

You could use the longer quotation in one paragraph, and **all** the shorter quotations in the other.

Putting it into practice

In Section A of your exam you will need to explore the presentational and structural features of a text and their effect. Read **Source 1** then look at the question on the next page.

Source 1

The secret footballer: undercover in the Premier League

Growing up on a council estate, all he wanted to do was play football. But a long career in the Premier League has made him question everything. Our Secret Footballer reveals what life is really like at the top of the game …

A few years ago, I seriously considered giving up football. Sometimes, when the games are coming thick and fast, and you don't see your family, you aren't playing wonderfully well and the results are poor, it gets on top of you. I would later come to realise this was depression knocking at the door.

As a kid, I played football day and night – I used to take a ball to bed with me so that I could do keep-ups as soon as I woke up. Football held the possibility of glory and happiness, and an escape from the mundane life that came with growing up in a small town. I played for the best local teams, the county and district sides, and was known in our area as one of a crop of talented players who were emerging.

When I eventually signed with a team (for £500 a week, which was a fortune to me), I set about my newfound career with the overriding feeling that they'd let someone in the door that perhaps they shouldn't have, an outsider into the inner sanctum. That feeling has never left me.

Putting it into practice

Look at the exam-style question below and read the extracts from two sample student answers.

Worked example

2 Explain how the headline, subheading and image are effective and how they link with the text. *(8 marks)*

Exploring presentational features

For a question like this you should:

- spend about 10–15 minutes
- read the source carefully and note how the presentational features link to and support its purpose, viewpoint and impact on the reader
- support all your points with evidence and a clear explanation focusing on effect.

Sample answer

The headline is in a big, bold font which grabs the reader's attention. The image is quite interesting because you can't really see the person in it. It's mysterious so it grabs the reader's attention. The subheading gives more information than the heading so it makes you want to read on.

✗ A vague comment needing much more detail and analysis to be effective.

✗ Another very general comment which does not focus on the language used or link back to the text in any way.

Make a note to avoid simplistic comments that do not link back to the text. The comments here could be about any headline.

Improved sample answer

The headline, subheading and picture all focus on the anonymity of the Secret Footballer. The key words in the headline are 'secret' and 'undercover' which suggest to the reader that the text will give them some inside information about the reality of life as a footballer in the Premier League: for example, the writer reveals his experience of 'depression' in the first few sentences which is surprising for someone who has achieved this level of success.

✓ An extremely effective opening comment, linking the three presentational features to the text.

✓ Identifies key language in the headline and comments on its effect.

✓ Clearly explains the headline's impact on the reader.

✓ Develops this idea further, clearly linking the headline to the text.

Now try this

Complete the 'Improved sample answer', focusing on the subheading and the image.

Remember to:

- avoid simplistic comments (e.g. 'grabs the reader's attention' and 'makes the reader want to read on')
- comment in detail on the use of language in the headline and subheading
- focus on the detail of the image and its effect
- link your comments back to the text.

Develop your explanations

It is important to select relevant points and effective evidence, but your explanations are where you answer the question and show how strong your reading skills are. You should aim to give an effective and developed explanation for each of your points and evidence.

Worked example

3 Read **Source 1**. Explain some of the writer's thoughts and feelings before, during and after this incident. *(8 marks)*

Sample answer

At the start of the extract, Grylls seems confident. He describes the jump he is about to make as 'Steep but manageable'. The word 'steep' suggests he recognises that it is dangerous, while the word 'manageable' is almost arrogant. The short sentence adds to this effect. It sounds like he is dismissing the danger in just three short words.

Notice how this explanation makes three very specific comments.

- Two of them focus on individual language choices, explaining their effect and how they influence the reader's perception of the writer.
- The third comments on the effect of the writer's choice of sentence structure.

Source 1

Mud, sweat and tears

'You set, buddy?' cameraman Simon asks me, smiling. His rig is all prepped and ready.

Beneath me is three hundred feet of steep snow and ice. Steep but manageable.

I leap.

I am soon traveling at over 40mph. Feet first down the mountain. The ice races past only inches from my head. This is my world.

I gain even more speed. The edge of the peak gets closer. Time to arrest the fall.

I flip nimbly onto my front and drive the ice axe into the snow. A cloud of white spray and ice soars into the air. It works like it always does. Like clockwork. Total confidence. I am now static.

The world hangs still. Then – bang.

Simon, his heavy wooden sled, plus solid metal camera housing, pile straight into my left thigh. He is doing in excess of 45mph.

There is an instant explosion of pain and noise and white.

It is like a freight train. And I am thrown down the mountain like a doll.

Now try this

Look again at **Source 1**. Write at least **one** further P-E-E paragraph which answers the exam-style question above.

- Remember to use linking phrases to connect your point, evidence and explanation.
- Aim to develop your explanation, commenting on at least two features of your chosen quotation.

Word classes

To help you comment on a writer's choice of language, think about the types of words they use.

Nouns

These are words used to describe:

- objects: e.g. table, building, dog, tree
- people: e.g. man, grandma, Ryan, mechanic
- places: e.g. town, countryside, London
- ideas: e.g. happiness, prejudice, religion.

Verbs

These are words used to describe:

- actions: e.g. to kick, to run, to fly
- occurrences: e.g. to fall, to collapse, to happen
- states: e.g. to be, to think, to wonder.

Remember: **pronouns** replace or stand in for nouns – e.g. I, you, he, our, theirs.

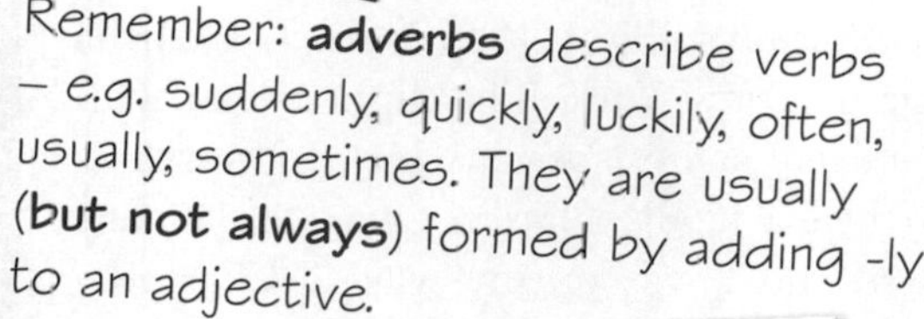

Remember: **adverbs** describe verbs – e.g. suddenly, quickly, luckily, often, usually, sometimes. They are usually (**but not always**) formed by adding -ly to an adjective.

Adjectives

These are words to describe a noun: e.g. good, red, large, nice, famous.

Remember: **adjectives** can become **comparatives** (e.g. better, larger) and **superlatives** (e.g. best, largest).

Comparatives and superlatives

Make sure you are familiar with these and how to use them.

Comparatives give degrees of difference: e.g. better, redder, nicer, more famous.

Superlatives give the most or least: e.g. best, reddest, nicest, most famous.

Examples

Here are some comments about the extracts opposite, focusing on word class:

1 

He crouches, springs, and flies, eventually crashing to the ground in a cloud of dust.

The writer uses a stream of action verbs to create a sense of urgent and dramatic movement.

2 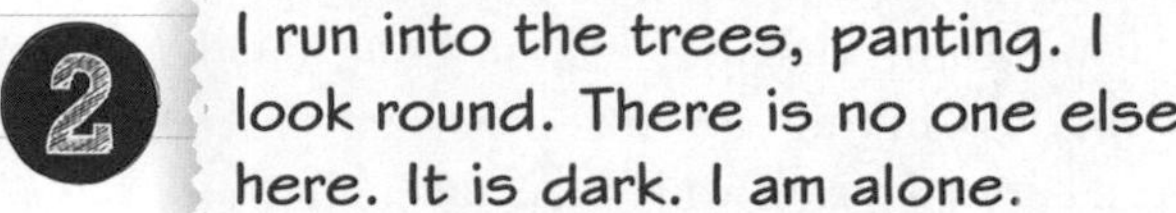

I run into the trees, panting. I look round. There is no one else here. It is dark. I am alone.

The writer focuses the reader on the pace of the action by using very few descriptive adverbs or adjectives.

3 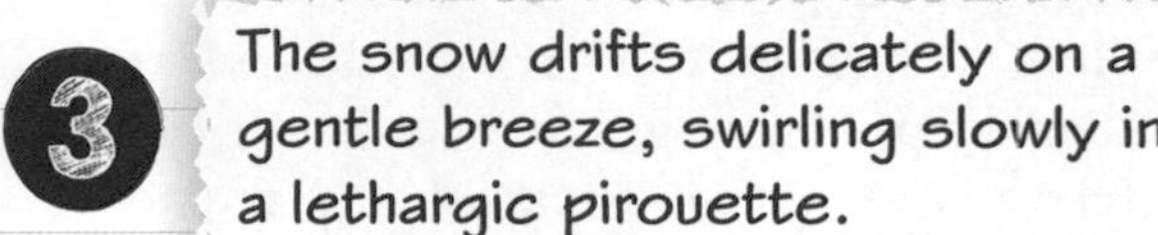

The snow drifts delicately on a gentle breeze, swirling slowly in a lethargic pirouette.

The writer paints a vivid picture with a rich choice of adjectives and adverbs.

Now try this

Write **one** sentence about **each** of these two extracts, focusing on word class and its effect.

The table groans with glistening green apples, hefty bowlfuls of muddy brown potatoes, and fluorescent red cherries.

Children come running, screaming, shouting, bawling and falling towards me.

Putting it into practice

In Section A, Question 3 of your exam, you must demonstrate that you can understand and infer meaning in a text. Read **Source 1** then look at the question on the next page.

Source 1

I crash-landed in the Hudson

I'VE NEVER been anxious about flying and was completely relaxed when I boarded US Airways flight 1549 from LaGuardia airport, New York. The flight began with the usual safety speech which I ignored as I'd heard it all before. It was 15 January 2009 and I was on my way to Charlotte, North Carolina, to see friends.

Within minutes of taking off, I heard the strangest popping sound coming from the engine, rather like a car backfiring. I certainly wouldn't have guessed the noise was down to a large flock of Canada geese flying into the plane's engines, disabling both of them on impact. My seat shook with the vibrations and suddenly the plane began dropping. Everything went eerily quiet – the familiar drone of the engines had disappeared. Gripping the armrests, I said to myself, 'OK, I am 27, I've never been married, but if it's my time to go, I'm OK with this.' A strange peace washed over me, one I've never experienced before or since. All my life I had struggled with anxiety and had learned coping techniques, but this was different.

Looking around, I noticed some passengers crying and others edging up in their seats to catch a glimpse out of the window. I locked eyes with the woman behind me. She was hyperventilating. A man a few seats down was making a phone call. Mostly everyone was quiet, except one passenger at the back who yelled, 'Fire!'

Moments later the captain announced: 'Brace for impact.' I had to figure out how to brace myself because, of course, I had never paid attention to the emergency drill. In the end, I grabbed the seat in front and held on tightly. The impact came with incredible force – I'm still amazed I walked away without any injuries. As we landed tail first, we were hurled back into our seats, then plunged forwards. Someone screamed, 'We're in water.' We all jumped to our feet, jostling towards the exit doors.

By now, water was rising as the back of the plane was submerged. I could hear people screaming and one instinct took over: the need to get out. By the time I reached the exit door, freezing water was up to my shins. I could see passengers standing outside on the icy wing. Aware of others behind me, I jumped into a life raft, soaking and shivering from the water and the wind howling down the river.

We waited for what felt like an hour, but was really only 10 minutes, before help arrived. We clambered into ferries and were taken first to a restaurant and then to a hotel. Over the next few days, airline staff bought me new clothes and a suitcase, and helped me to get a new passport.

Two days later I was on another plane to Charlotte. I found it a little unnerving, but I was keen to overcome any fear I might have. When faced with anxiety, I'm comforted when I recall the peace I felt on flight 1549 – and I definitely pay closer attention to the safety procedures now.

Putting it into practice

Look at the exam-style question below and read the two sample student answers.

Worked example

3 Explain some of the writer's thoughts and feelings before, during and after the crash. *(8 marks)*

Understanding and inferring meaning

For a question like this you should:

- spend about 10–15 minutes
- read the source carefully and highlight relevant words, phrases and sentences
- support all your points with evidence and a clear explanation focusing on **effect**.

Sample answer

The writer says she has never been anxious about flying. Like most people she did not pay any attention to the safety speech at the start of the flight.

The writer describes a strange noise and the plane is dropping. The only detail the writer gives which suggests her fear as the plane starts to drop is when she describes herself 'gripping the armrests' – and even though she says she felt 'a strange peace', this does suggest she is terrified.

You should avoid making points that are not relevant. Here, the answer should focus on thoughts and feelings **before**, **during** and **after** the crash.

✗ The relevance of this point to the writer's thoughts and feelings is not made clear.

✓ These valid points comment on inference, supported with evidence.

Improved sample answer

The overall impression of the writer's thoughts and feelings is that she is calm throughout the whole incident. At the start of the flight she is 'relaxed' and even when she hears a 'strange popping sound', her seat 'shook' and the plane started 'dropping', the only suggestion of fear is that she was 'gripping the armrests'. This is almost immediately dismissed as she accepts she may die and feels 'a strange peace'. She then reveals that 'All my life I had struggled with anxiety' which makes this, and her apparent calmness throughout the crash, all the more surprising – perhaps even hard to believe.

✓ An effective introduction focusing on the overall impression of the writer's thoughts and feelings in the text.

✓ Effective use of embedded quotations contrasting the frightening situation with the limited description of her feelings.

✓ Develops the idea further, and perceptively questions the writer's consistency and honesty in describing her feelings.

Now try this

Complete the 'Improved sample answer', aiming to identify at least **two** more relevant points.

Remember to:

- check that all your points focus on the writer's thoughts and feelings
- support all your points with carefully chosen quotations and detailed explanations.

Had a look ☐ Nearly there ☐ Nailed it! ☐

Connotations

Some words can create bigger ideas in our minds through the ideas and attitudes they suggest. These ideas and attitudes are called **connotations**.

Thinking about what a word or phrase suggests can help you to write effective comments on the writer's choice of language.

Look at what the word 'squeaked' could suggest in the example opposite.

'Help!' I squeaked.

The connotation of the word 'squeaked' suggests the narrator or writer is like a mouse. This, in turn, suggests they might be small, timid and frightened.

Language choice

These sentences have similar literal meanings. But the connotations let you know the writer's **real attitude**.

1. An unfamiliar aroma wafts through the air.
2. A strange smell fills the air.
3. A weird stench seeps through the air.

If you explore the connotations of a writer's language choice, it can help you write about their attitude.

Source 1

Freak shows

Our TV screens are filled nightly with otherwise obscure people who suffer gross physical deformities. The justification for exposing them is that making public the difficulties of such lives is a healthy, cathartic process. But are the producers' motives any better than those who ran freak shows in Victorian times, as depicted in *The Elephant Man?* The TV shows pull in a lowing herd of undiscerning viewers who, in turn, attract advertising from firms which prosper by targeting them.

Read **Source 1** opposite. The writer conveys his viewpoint through the connotations of the language he has chosen.

This literally means **large** or **extreme**, but also carries connotations of revulsion.

This literally means **showing** or **revealing**, but also has connotations suggesting being made vulnerable, perhaps to ridicule or embarrassment.

This refers to people with deformities who were put on display for misguided visitors' entertainment. It has strong connotations of exploitation.

Now try this

1 Look again at **Source 1**. What are the connotations of the words underlined in blue above:
- lowing herd
- targeting?

2 Write a sentence about the word, commenting on what the writer is suggesting with his choice of language.

3 Write **two** or **three** sentences about the writer's attitude to viewers of these kinds of television programmes.

Rhetorical devices 1

You will need to think about the range of language or rhetorical devices that writers use to emphasise their point or manipulate the reader's response.

Comment on rhetorical devices

To improve your exam responses you will need to **comment on** the effect of rhetorical devices. Here are some examples.

Alliteration: two or more words close to each other that begin with the same sound. Can be used to emphasise an idea.

The writer uses alliteration in the title, emphasising the key point of the text.

Rhetorical question: a question used to engage the reader.

Opening the article with a rhetorical question immediately engages the reader, encouraging them to ask themselves the question and keep reading to discover the answer.

Pattern of three: a rhythmic trio of words or phrases used for emphasis.
Synonym: a word or phrase that means the same as another word or phrase.

The writer uses a pattern of three synonyms to highlight how busy London is.

Repetition: a repeated word or phrase to emphasise an idea.

Repetition emphasises how different London is to the rest of the country.

Lists: a series of items or ideas, often used to highlight quantity or variety.

The writer draws our attention to the pace and variety of life in London with a long list.

Source 1

London welcomes the world

Why is our capital so busy, active and bustling? The same cannot be said of the nation as a whole. But London is different. London is a competitive Babel of commercial interests, immigrant populations, national politics, artistic energy, media, administration, monarchy, students and tourists. Because of the English language and its large (though poorly run) airports, it is a hub for half the globe. It is hard to think of anything you could not buy there or anyone you could not meet. More than of any other city today, you can say of London that if you have not been there, you have not really seen the world.

Whatever the fluctuating fortunes of the rest of Britain, the activity never stops. People who live in London get cynical about all the praise heaped on its 'buzz' and 'vibrancy'. These can be codewords for drugs, late-night noise and multi-culturalism run riot. It may be difficult that so many citizens of the world seek refuge, or fame, or fortune, in our grimy capital, but it is, broadly speaking, a compliment that they do so. Better to welcome the world than to hide from it.

Now try this

Look at the second paragraph in **Source 1.** Identify as many other examples of rhetorical devices as you can. Write **one** or **two** sentences about the effect each one is intended to have on the reader.

Remember, an answer that **comments on the effect** of a rhetorical device is better than one that only names the device.

Rhetorical devices 2

You will need to think about how writers use a range of language or rhetorical devices to emphasise their point or manipulate the reader's response.

Comment on rhetorical devices

To improve your exam responses you will need to **comment on** the effect of rhetorical devices. Here are some examples.

Remember to comment on, rather than just name, the devices.

Emotive language: words intended to create an extreme response or play on the reader's emotions.

The writer uses emotive language to suggest that young people are terrified disabled by their fear of failure.

Hyperbole: exaggeration used to make a point.

The writer uses hyperbole to emphasise young people's expectations, suggesting that they are totally unrealistic.

Contrast: comparing two opposing or different ideas to emphasise the difference between them.

The writer repeatedly contrasts today's young people with other groups to make her point.

A short sentence: a short punchy sentence used to emphasise a dramatic point.

The writer finishes on a short sentence, summarising her point in a hard-hitting and dramatic conclusion.

Source 2

Why so many children are failing to grow up

Throughout school, I worked every Saturday and every holiday. My generation was obsessed with work: we wanted to earn money, to have good careers, to make something of our lives. And we were prepared to start at the bottom to do so.

Our children, by contrast, have a sense of entitlement coupled with a paralysing fear of failure. It starts with the pressure we put them under to succeed academically: in consequence, many of them work hard at school and strive to get into good universities.

But having achieved the academic success that was demanded of them, they are bemused not to be offered the world on a plate.

In countries where it's still considered normal to strive, you won't hear it much discussed. Chinese and Indian children are in no doubt about why they're working so hard at school: in order to enter careers that enable them not only to raise their own families but to take care of their parents, too.

Our children, by contrast, have been raised in an infantilising culture that tells them nothing should be unfair or hard or uncomfortable. Of course some of them haven't grown up. They haven't been taught how to.

Now try this

Look at **Source 2**. Identify as many other examples of rhetorical device as you can. Write **one** or **two** sentences about the effect each one is intended to have on the reader.

EXAM SKILL

Make sure you are familiar with these devices:
- alliteration
- rhetorical question
- pattern of three
- list
- repetition
- contrast
- hyperbole
- emotive language
- short sentences

Use this skill to help you improve the quality of your writing.

Figurative language

You will need to remember that figurative language (also known as **imagery**) is used to create an image in the reader's mind.

Comment on figurative language

To improve your exam responses you will need to **comment on** the effect of figurative language in a text.

Remember to comment on, rather than just name, figurative language.

Here are some examples.

Simile: a comparison, usually using 'as' or 'like', suggesting a resemblance between one thing and another – e.g. Her bedroom was like a prison.

The writer uses a simile to compare the size of the icebergs to the size of the ship. This not only gives the reader a sense of how huge they are but also makes them more threatening by suggesting they could overpower the ship in some way.

Metaphor: a direct comparison suggesting a resemblance between one thing and another – e.g. Her bedroom was a prison.

The writer uses a metaphor comparing the icebergs to jewels. This suggests that they are rare, precious, valuable and beautiful.

Personification: describing something non-human as if it were human – e.g. The leaves danced in the breeze.

The writer personifies the icebergs as placid giants suggesting their size but also hinting at the danger which they threaten.

Source 1

The white jewels of the Atlantic

We were on a summer cruise along the Greenland coast, nudging our way past lumps of floating ice ranging from 'growlers' the size of a car to bergs almost as large as ships. It was the white jewels of ice floating serenely past the ship that most commanded our attention. Some, like vast uncut diamonds, were almost transparent.

It seemed a simple proposition to pull up alongside, leap across and explore these placid giants. They looked stable enough. Then a berg the size of our boat rolled completely over. The resultant waves made us hold on to the boat's rail and we saw why our skipper had exercised great caution in his navigation through the ice.

Eventually, as a floating white blanket of ice blocked our course, the engine was cut and a profound silence descended. Then an ice fragment was scooped from the water and a crew member began to smash it with a hammer. The ice sparkled in our glasses as we raised them in a toast to the crew and their boat, to the Greenlanders and their vast and beautiful land.

Now try this

Look at **Source 1**. Identify at least **two** more examples of figurative language. Write **one** or **two** sentences about the effect each example is intended to have on the reader.

Remember: an answer that **comments on the effect** of figurative language will gain more marks than one which simply says 'it's a simile'.

Identifying sentence types

Make sure you can recognise the four basic types of sentence: simple, complex, compound and minor.

Simple sentences

These contain a subject and **one verb**. So they give **one piece of information** about an event or action. For example:

The dog chased the ball.

This is the verb.

Complex sentences

These are longer sentences with one part dependent on another. So they contain **two or more verbs** and give **two or more pieces of information**. The piece that is most important is called the **main clause**. The other piece is called the **subordinating** or **dependent** clause, because it needs the main clause to make sense. For example:

The dog chased the ball until it was exhausted.

This is the main clause.

This is the subordinating clause.

Note how the two clauses are joined with connecting words such as **because**, **although** and **if**. In this example, the connecting word is **until**.

Sometimes, the two clauses in a complex sentence can be swapped round. For example:

Until it was exhausted, the dog chased the ball.

Compound sentences

These are a series of simple sentences joined together. So they contain **two or more verbs** and give **two or more pieces** of information about events or actions. For example:

The dog chased the ball and brought it back.

These are the verbs.

Note how the pieces of information are joined with words such as **and**, **but** and **then**. In this example, the connecting word is **and**.

Minor sentences

These are grammatically incomplete because they do not contain a verb. For example:

Poor dog. Yes. So what?

Now try this

What kind of sentences are these? How do you know?

1 Because he fell over, the child burst into tears.
2 He cried and cried.
3 He howled like a wolf.
4 When he finally stopped, his father smiled.
5 The father put the child to bed and listened carefully at his bedroom door.
6 Silence.

Commenting on sentence types

You will need to remember that **how** writers structure a sentence can have just as much impact on the reader as the **language** they choose.

Sentences and audience

Different sentence types can reflect a text's target reader. Look at these examples.

A text aimed at younger children will use more (and sometimes nothing but) short simple sentences:

Sally wants to play catch. She goes in the garden. The sun is shining.

A complex text aimed at adults will use a variety of sentence types including longer, complex sentences:

While European unity may be desirable for many politicians, it does not always appeal to members of the voting public who may feel that it represents a loss of nationhood and of independence.

Sentence and mood

Sentences can reflect the mood the writer is trying to create. Look at these examples.

A longer complex sentence can suggest time dragging:

We sat and we waited, watching the clock, tapping our toes, drumming our fingers anxiously on our knees, then pacing the floor until finally it was our turn.

A series of shorter sentences can suggest anxiety and build tension:

I stopped. I listened. I heard nothing.

Long and short sentences

Short, simple sentences can be used for dramatic effect. This can be accentuated when the short simple sentence follows a longer sentence. Look at these examples.

Running through the woods, I darted between the trees, one eye always over my shoulder, the other peering into the distant darkness, scouring the shadows. Then I saw him.

Notice how the final short sentence provides a sudden and dramatic conclusion to the tension-building of the longer sentence.

Many people are under the impression that GCSEs have become so easy that success is simply a matter of turning up, with or without a pen. They are wrong.

Notice how the final short sentence sharply dismisses the argument presented in the longer sentence.

Now try this

Choose any source text from any page of this guide. Find **three** sentences that the writer of that text has structured for effect. Write **one** or **two** sentences about the effect of each one.

Remember to look out for unusual sentence construction: short or long sentences, or a text consisting mainly of one type of sentence. Think: why has the writer done this? What effect is intended?

Putting it into practice

In Section A, Question 4 of your exam, you will need to write about the ways language is used in texts. Read **Source 1** then look at the question on the next page. Note that in your exam you will be asked to **compare** the ways in which language is used in two texts. Use this question to practise writing about language in just **one** text.

Source 1

Decoding Dad

I perplexed my father because I was so unlike him. He couldn't comprehend my need for books. I was not what he expected. He believed I'd become his mirror image: stout and brawny, adept at physical lifting and with a head for mental arithmetic. He saw no point in 'made-up novels' or poetry. The towers of books in my bedroom flummoxed him. Without football we'd have had nothing to say to each other.

People are like rivers. To understand them properly you have to find their source, a realisation that in my father's case came too late to be useful to me. This is what I know about the man who everyone called Jim or Jimmy. He worked, aged 12 to 14, in a bakery. From 14 he took the only road open to him. He went into the pit and stayed there. Escape was impossible.

In the 1960s he dragged his miner's kit from Newcastle to Nottingham because the seam of the pit in which he worked was exhausted. He said goodbye to Newcastle with the reluctance and resentment of a refugee. Every summer we went back there. For one thing, we could only afford to holiday at my grandfather's home, which was three miles from the coast. For another, my father didn't want to go anywhere else. He wanted the Geordie air in his lungs.

He demonstrated faithfulness towards everything Geordie. The first of these was to Newcastle United. Football was at the centre of everything to my father.

He bought me copies of *Goal* magazine. He returned home with a once-a-week packet of football stickers, which he propped up on the mantelpiece. And the day after my grandfather's funeral he offered something to help me forget, however fleetingly, the ache of his loss.

I was sitting dejectedly on the sofa when he appeared carrying my limp coat. 'We're going into the Toon,' he said. 'The two of us. I'll buy you a Newcastle shirt. We'll get a badge for it and a number 9 to stitch on the back.'

In my boyhood, a replica kit was neither ubiquitous nor cheap. The inside of the shop was as dark as a cave. The middle-aged man serving us wore a poorly fitting grey suit and had fingers as thin as splinters. He measured us sullenly with his eyes, as if our entrance was a disturbance to him. He found a shirt, held it against my chest and announced it was the right size. The badge and the poppy red number 9 on a rectangle of white cloth came separately. My father reached inside his wallet and produced a £10 note.

Saying nothing as he did so, the assistant wrapped everything in brown paper, and then wove a line of coarse string around the parcel. He passed it to my father, who passed it on to me. 'You'll be champion in that,' my father said.

There would be occasions in the future – and a lot of them too – when my father would frustrate or infuriate me because of his reticence, his detachment and his apparent lack of tenderness towards me. But, whenever I was in danger of mistaking it for ambivalence, I'd remember that football shirt. And I think of it whenever I hear anyone say, dismissively, that football doesn't matter; or that football is just a game; or even 'Well, it's only football.'

No, it isn't. Not for me. It bound us together when nothing else could. Without football, we were strangers under a shared roof. With it, we were father and son.

Putting it into practice

Look at this exam-style question and read the two sample student answers.

Writing about language

For a question like this you should:

- spend about 10–15 minutes
- read the source carefully and note effective use of language
- support all your points with evidence and a clear explanation focusing on **effect**.

Worked example

4 Explore the different ways in which language is used for effect in **Source 1**.

Give some examples and analyse the effects. (In your exam you will be asked to compare **two** texts.) *(16 marks)*

Sample answer

The writer says he doesn't understand his dad:

'I perplexed my father because I was so unlike him.'

The word 'perplexed' shows that the writer and his father were not close. It was only football that gave them something to talk about. Otherwise they had nothing in common.

The writer uses a simile to compare people to rivers. This imagery creates a picture in the reader's mind.

✗ The writer implies he does not understand his dad, but this is not supported by the evidence given which suggests that his dad did not understand him.

✗ Although this explanation develops the point and mentions the writer's language choice, it does not offer detailed comment on its effect.

If you name a language feature, then comment fully on its effect. The comment here is very simplistic.

Improved sample answer

The opening paragraph of the text focuses on the gap between father and son. The words 'perplexed' and 'flummoxed' emphasise the lack of understanding between father and son.

This distance is further emphasised but also reduced by the short simple sentence of the opening paragraph: 'Without football we'd have had nothing to say to each other.' The short, blunt word 'nothing' makes the reader realise just how fragile the bond was between parent and child and the importance of football in their relationship.

Notice how this summing up shows a clear understanding of the text.

✓ Supported with embedded evidence focusing closely on language choice with a comment on its effect.

✓ A second point develops the idea, focusing on sentence structure

✓ A longer quotation, supported with careful analysis, focusing on language and effect again

Now try this

Complete the 'Improved sample answer', aiming to identify at least **two** more relevant points.

Remember to focus on specific language choices and comment closely on their effect.

Making the best comments

The depth and detail of your comments on a writer's choices can make a real difference to the quality of your answer.

Read this exam-style question and **Source 1**.

Worked example

3 Explain some of the writer's thoughts and feelings about her appearance and her achievements. *(8 marks)*

Source 1

As a teenager I was horribly thin, had a mouth full of big frilly teeth, wore unflattering National Health glasses and was cursed with drab, beige hair that refused to curl, no matter what my mother did to it.

That was the external packaging – but inside, I was 100 per cent rebel. Mother Nature might have given me unpromising raw material, but I realised at 12 that my brain – not the size of my bust – was my ultimate weapon.

1 You could start your answer with some evidence:

At the start of the article, the writer describes herself when she was younger as 'horribly thin' and 'cursed with drab, beige hair'.

Now you need to **explain** the writer's thoughts and feelings, and how they are conveyed.

To explain the point and evidence above, you could comment on:

- viewpoint

The writer focuses the reader on her appearance before dismissing it as unimportant.

- purpose

With this negative self-portrait, the writer uses extreme honesty to win the reader over to her argument.

- language choice

The word 'cursed' suggests this was one of the worst things that could possibly happen to her.

- sentence structure

This long sentence listing a range of negative features emphasises how disappointed the writer was with every aspect of her appearance.

- effect on the reader

The use of humour engages the reader immediately.

Remember, you can make comments on any combination of these five things.

Now try this

Write a second point about **Source 1**. Support it with evidence from the text. Then write **five** different comments focusing on: viewpoint, purpose, language choice, sentence structure and effect on the reader.

Comment on language and purpose: argue and persuade

You can develop the detail and depth of your explanation if you link your comment on language to the purpose of the text – in this case, to **argue** and **persuade**.

Argument and persuasive texts

These texts use a range of language features to **influence** the reader's **opinions** and **actions**. For example:

- newspaper articles – the writer expresses their opinion, trying to convince the reader to agree
- advertisements – they try to persuade the reader to buy a product or service
- charity appeals – they try to persuade the reader to support their cause.

Look out for, and comment on, the key features of argument and persuasion in texts like these.

How writers do it

Writers argue and persuade by using **rhetorical devices** such as:

- rhetorical questions
- emotive language
- hyperbole
- contrast
- lists
- repetition.

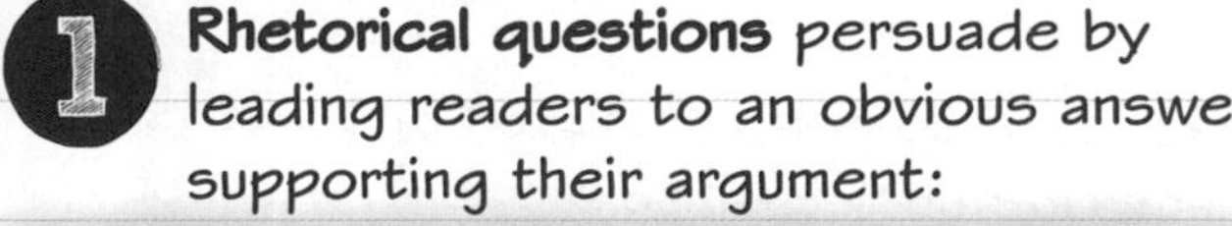

1 **Rhetorical questions** persuade by leading readers to an obvious answer supporting their argument:

> Would you like to make a lot of money for doing almost nothing?

2 **Emotive language** influences the reader's view of a particular idea or situation:

> A **crisis** sounds much more serious than a **problem**.

3 **Hyperbole** (or exaggeration) emphasise a key point, or create humour to win the reader over:

> The world is facing the greatest crisis in its entire history.

4 **Contrast** emphasises the negative or positive elements in an argument.

> You have everything.

> He has nothing.

Notice how a contrast like this could persuade you to help someone more disadvantaged than you.

5 **Lists** are used to demonstrate the range or appeal of ideas in an argument. For example, this list emphasises just how useful this product is for everyone.

> This product is great for men, women, children, and even pets!

6 **Repeating** a word or phrase effectively hammers home the point the writer wants to make. For example:

> Of all the mad ideas in our mad world, this is the maddest.

Now try this

Choose **two** source texts from this guide that argue or persuade. How many **rhetorical devices** can you identify in them? Write a sentence commenting on the effect of each one.

Had a look ☐ Nearly there ☐ Nailed it! ☐

Comment on language and purpose: describe

You can develop the detail and depth of your explanation by linking your comment on language to the purpose of the text – in this case, to **describe**.

Descriptive texts

Descriptive texts use a range of features to **create a picture** in the reader's mind. For example:

- travel writing – describes a place or a journey
- autobiographical writing – describes an event or experience.

Look out for, and comment on, the key features of description in texts like these.

How writers do it

Writers describe by using:

- language choice
- figurative language
- the five senses
- feelings

Language choice is made very carefully. A writer thinks hard about connotation and its impact on the reader.

I perched precariously on my sledge as we hurtled across the frozen wasteland.

I sat on my sledge as we went over the ice.

Get used to commenting on descriptive language choice. For example, in the first sentence the writer suggests danger (**perched**), speed (**hurtled**) and a hostile environment (**wasteland**).

The five senses cover descriptions of sight, sound, smell, touch and taste.

Remember that you can comment on **either** individual examples of sensory description **or** the quantity of sensory description the writer uses in the text.

Figurative language creates a picture in the reader's mind through the use of imagery or figurative language. For example:

- similes
- metaphor
- personification.

Remember to comment on the effect of the figurative language and what it suggests to the reader.

4

Feelings are often described using their physical effect on the writer. This helps the reader imagine how that feeling really feels. For example:

My heart thumped and my mouth went dry. I was terrified.

Remember that a writer is trying to create tension for the reader, so they will read on to see what happened.

Now try this

Choose **two** source texts from this guide which describe. How many key descriptive features can you identify in them? Write a sentence commenting on the effect of each one.

Comment on language and purpose: inform and explain

You can develop the detail and depth of your explanation by linking your comment on language to the purpose of the text – in this case, to **inform** and **explain**.

Information and explanation texts

Information texts include:
- encyclopedia entries
- fact sheets
- reports.

They aim to present the reader with facts.

Explanation texts include:
- instruction manuals
- school textbooks
- any text that answers the questions 'How?' and 'Why?'.

How writers do it

Information and explanation texts do not use as many language features as persuasive or descriptive texts. Instead, writers use other features such as:
- structure
- tone
- facts
- statistics.

Get used to looking out for and commenting on the effect of these features.

1 **Structure**

Information and explanation texts **do** follow a logical structure, often in chronological order. To signpost this to the reader, they sometimes use connectives such as:
- First, …
- Next …
- Then …
- Finally, …

2 **Tone**

Some explanation and information texts use informal language to appeal to their intended audience, e.g. a leaflet aimed at teenagers may use more abbreviations and slang. More often, they have a formal tone or register. To achieve this, they use:
- formal language
- standard English
- the third person (he, she, they).

Note that these suggest the information is impartial, unbiased, accurate and reliable.

3 **Facts and statistics**

Information and explanation texts often use a range of facts and statistics to achieve their purpose. They highlight key facts like this:

> In the last year, nearly 2,000 people have been killed on Britain's roads.

Facts and statistics convey to the reader that the text, and the information or explanation it gives, can be trusted and relied upon.

Now try this

Choose **two** source texts from this guide that inform or explain. Look at **Source 2** on page 47 and **Source 2** on page 50. How many of the key features on this page can you identify in them? Write a sentence commenting on the effect of each one.

Had a look ☐ Nearly there ☐ Nailed it! ☐

Putting it into practice

In Section A, Question 4 of your exam, you will need to write about the ways language is used in texts. Read **Source 1** then look at the question on the next page. (Note that in your exam you will be asked to **compare** the ways in which language is used in two texts. Use this question to practise writing about language in just **one** text.)

Source 1

The poverty of a generation deprived of the natural wonders of my 'free range' childhood

If you wanted to make a list of things to have done by the time you reach your teens, I should have thought it might have included things like 'learn French', 'go skiing', 'learn to surf', so wide is the world of children these days.

But no, so housebound are they in reality, shackled to their computers, TV sets, Xboxes and other accessories of the high wired generation, that the National Trust has made a list of all the things we used to do to inspire today's young to have a go.

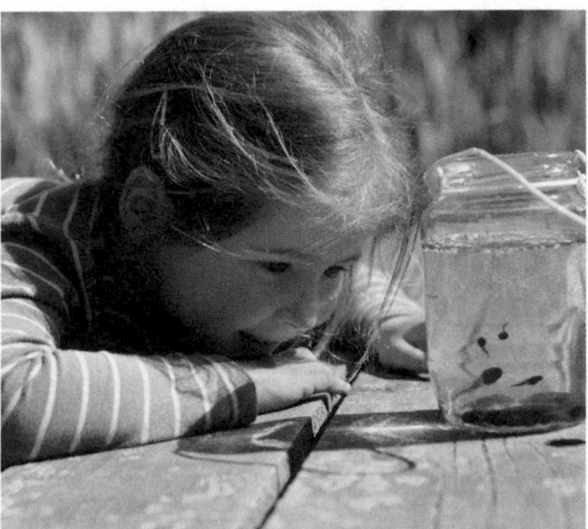

Skim a stone, run around in the rain, play conkers, make a mud pie.

There was nothing else to do, before the microchip, so that's what we did and many other simple pleasures beside and it didn't do us any harm.

I was the original free range child. I was never at home if I could help it, but on the common or even the streets. From the age of seven, perhaps even earlier, I was on my bike or up a tree. I fell from a top branch while pretending to be a bird and off a high fence while following a cat. My brother severed his finger in a bicycle chain which he was trying to put back in place.

I went camping and ended up in hospital when the tent was washed away in a deluge. None of these tiny mishaps stopped us and we are still here to tell the tale.

I caught crabs and dug for coins on the Mersey estuary and as for sledging (also on the list) I had something much better – an all-weather go-kart. Knocked together out of two bicycle wheels and old tea crate with a chair handle bound with insulating tape for a brake, I would take it out after breakfast, get lost in the woods and not return till sundown. I kept up my strength by blackberrying. That's another thing on the list and it remains one of my favourite pastimes.

As for frog spawn – the list includes that – I remember a whole pond of it which we regularly plundered in spring taking it back in jam jars with a piece of string round the top. We watched the tadpoles hatch and grow into frogs and released them into the back garden. Who does that these days, partly because today's children would be hard pushed to recognise a tadpole, let alone find one.

'The outdoors is a treasure trove,' as Fiona Reynolds of the National Trust says. Lighting a campfire, cooking, canoeing, bug-hunting, rolling around in the grass … what wonderful memories each of the 50 items brings back now. Although we had practically no material riches, how enormously privileged we were – and wouldn't it be nice if a new generation could see things that way.

Putting it into practice

Look at the exam-style question below and read the two sample student answers.

Worked example

4 Compare the different ways in which language is used for effect in **Source 1**.
Give some examples and analyse the effects. (In your exam you will be asked to compare **two** texts.) *(16 marks)*

Writing about language

For a question like this you should:

- spend about 10–15 minutes
- read the source carefully and note effective use of language
- support all your points with evidence and a clear explanation focusing on **effect**.

Sample answer

The article is written in the first person so this is obviously a very personal point of view. The writer doesn't seem to understand that not everyone wants to go skiing, or that it is actually possible to go skiing and play on an Xbox, maybe even on the same day!

She describes herself as a 'free range' child which, although it suggests chickens, is here meant to suggest freedom and health and well-being. It also suggests that those people who are shut up inside their houses watching TV or playing on computers are like battery hens: mistreated and knowing no better.

✓ A reasonable point supported with limited analysis.

✗ This responds to the writer's viewpoint effectively but does not comment on the writer's choice of language and therefore does not answer the question.

Note how effective this analysis of connotation is. It is developed further with an effective analysis of the writer's implication.

Improved sample answer

To support her argument, the writer uses a number of lists in the text. She contrasts her ideas of what teenagers might want to do such as 'learn French, go skiing', with a list of typical teenage obsessions including 'computers, tv sets, Xboxes'. With these lists, she compares and contrasts what teenagers could do, what they used to do, and what they actually do. This highlights how disappointed she is in them. She emphasises this with the word 'shackled' as though teenagers are being kept prisoner by the technology which keeps them 'housebound'.

Note how this answer identifies the purpose of the text and the language features that support it.

✓ Effective comment on rhetorical device – i.e. contrast – supported with short, embedded quotations.

✓ A perceptive comment on effect, along with a close focus on specific language choice.

Now try this

Complete the 'Improved sample answer', aiming to identify at least **two** more relevant points.

Remember to focus on specific language choices and comment closely on their effect.

Looking closely at language

Section A, Question 4, asks you to compare the different ways in which language is used in two sources and analyse its effects.

Questioning the source texts

Before you can answer Question 4, you need to look **very** closely at the source texts and **question** the language the writer has chosen to use. You could ask yourself:

Choosing the source texts

In the exam, you may be **told** which two texts to compare. **but** if you are asked to **choose**, make sure you explore each text carefully before deciding which you can compare most successfully.

Remember: you will need to write about **two** texts in the exam.

- **What is the purpose of the text?** Does the language help the text achieve it?

This article's main purpose is to persuade the reader to consider animal welfare. In doing this it also uses descriptive language.

- **What types and lengths of sentences has the writer used?** What effect do they have?

The writer begins the article with a short, blunt, simple sentence suggesting his personal opinion is indisputable.

Source 1

Can't resist a bacon sandwich?

There is something irresistible about the smell of fried bacon. For some, the joy of bacon lies in rashers squeezed between factory-sliced white bread and smeared with tomato ketchup.

For others, it's the crisp slice of streaky bacon on the British breakfast plate, ready to be dipped into a runny yellow yolk or a dollop of baked beans.

But are those rashers that sizzle so seductively in the pan what they seem?

For every slice of high quality, dry cured bacon from a happy organic British pig, there are many more imported from countries where pigs endure overcrowded, barbaric conditions and where the meat is pumped with water and injected with cancer-causing chemicals.

- **What tone has the writer created?** How has the writer's choice of language helped create this?

The descriptive language in the first two paragraphs creates a positive tone through appeal to the senses.

- **What techniques has the writer used?** Look out for the language techniques you revised on pages 38–40. What effect do they have in this text?

However the tone of the article changes with a rhetorical question, inviting the reader to consider animal welfare.

Emotive language is used to shock the reader.

Now try this

Identify **two** further points you could make about the writer's choice of language in **Source 1**. Write a sentence about each one, commenting on its effect.

Remember to **comment** on effects, rather than list what they are.

Planning to compare language

Of all the questions in Section A, Question 4 is the most challenging and worth the most marks. You will write a much better answer if you spend 4 or 5 minutes planning it.

Planning

One way to plan your answer is to read both texts carefully and note down the purpose of each text, the language techniques used and the effects they create. You can then identify some similarities and differences to explore.

Source 1

Guardian Holiday Offers

MURDER MYSTERY ON THE SEVERN VALLEY STEAM RAILWAY

A fun-filled short break to die for!

Picture the scene: The Severn Valley Railway's vintage steam train chugs its way through spectacular Worcestershire countryside. You're on board, enjoying a delicious three-course meal. But there's a twist to this tranquil tale – there's a murderer on the train, and it's up to you and your fellow guests to find out whodunnit!

Persuasive

- Commands: 'Picture the scene', engages the reader.
- Positive language to persuade: 'spectacular … delicious … tranquil'.
- Exclamation marks: excitement.
- Direct address: 'you're on board'.
- Emotive language: 'twist', 'murderer'.

Source 2

Why do the elderly often fall for the 'too good to be true' scams?

Email pop-ups, letters offering a lottery win in exchange for bank details and cold callers ringing with a too-good-to-be-true deal. They all seem such an obvious scam to the majority.

But while most dismiss the offers as spam, many elderly people are duped by the con artists.

Now a study claims it is because a specific area of the brain has deteriorated or is damaged.

Researchers say they have discovered the exact part of the brain, called the ventromedial prefrontal cortex (vmPFC), that controls belief and doubt. As people get older the vmPFC deteriorates.

Informative

- Pattern of three: 'pop-ups, letters, cold callers' engages reader.
- Scientific language to inform: 'ventromedial prefrontal cortex'.
- Emotive language: 'duped', 'con artists'.

Now try this

Look at these sentence starters. Use each one to write a paragraph comparing the language techniques in the two sources and their topic effects.

1 Both texts use language to engage the reader from the start …
2 Both texts use emotive language …
3 Both texts use language choice to achieve their purpose …

EXAM SKILL

When comparing the language in two texts use Point-Evidence-Explain paragraphs so that you can:

- support each point with evidence from each text
- explain in detail the effects of the writers' language choices and their impact on the reader.

Use this skill to help you improve the quality of your writing.

Comparing language

Section A, Question 4 asks you to compare the different ways in which language is used in two sources and analyse its effects.

Comparing language

When you **compare** the use of language and its effects in two texts:

- **do** make direct comparisons between language features and their effect
- **don't** simply write about the language in one text and then the language in the other text.

Source 1

Andy Murray: not miserable, just normal

People say Murray's miserable because he doesn't smile very often. He's not miserable. He's normal. Have you walked down a street recently? Any street in the country? Go on, pick one. Take a stroll. Bring a notepad. Make a note each time you spot someone walking around beaming. Chances are you'll cross six postcodes before you glimpse so much as a smirk. Which isn't to say people are inherently unhappy. Just that they've got better things to do with their faces than walking around bending their mouths up like idiots.

Source 2

What makes me happy

Despite popular opinion regarding the degenerate youth who roam Britain's streets looking for fights and throwing up everywhere, it appears that teenagers are, in fact, the happiest people in the country.

Don't get me wrong, a high percentage of my weekly happiness comes from fighting and throwing up everywhere, but there are other things that make me happy.

The guest appearances of the sun is one – but one which also causes mass upheaval to any student's schedule. Anything and everything must be done in the park. Even revision. Especially revision. Unless, of course, you're a first-year English student and you don't have any exams.

1 You can **either** compare similar language features in the two texts and explore their effect ...

Both **Source 1** and **Source 2** texts engage the reader by directly addressing them.

Or you can compare similar effects created by different language techniques.

Source 1 creates humour using aggressive, blunt commands.

Source 2 creates humour through hyperbole.

Now try this

1 Identify **one** further language technique used in both texts.

2 Write **two** paragraphs comparing the use of language and its effects in the two sources.

Answering a compare question

Writing about and comparing two texts is difficult. You will fully demonstrate your understanding if you use an effective structure for your answer.

Structure

Aim to make direct comparisons.

You could **focus on one language feature** or its effect in the first text, then compare it to a similar feature or effect in the second text.

You could also **explore differences** – for example, writing about the different tones of the two texts and how language is used to achieve them.

Connectives

Use connectives to signpost the way through your answer.

For example, you could **signpost a similarity** using connectives like: 'Similarly ...' or 'In the same way ...'

To **signpost a difference** you can use connectives like: 'However ...' or 'Whereas ...'

Worked example

Write a brief introduction in one sentence summarising the two texts and their purposes.

Both texts are about ... but **Source 1** aims to ... while **Source 2** tries to ...

Write about a language feature in **Source 1**, supported with evidence and an explanation of its effect on the reader.

Source 1 uses ...

Similarly, **Source 2** uses ...

Use a connective to link a point about a similar language feature in **Source 2**. Support this with evidence and explanation as well.

Both texts use emotive language. For example, **Source 1** ...

This makes the reader realise that ...

On the other hand, **Source 2** uses emotive language to achieve a different effect ...

EXAM SKILL

Remember that you can write about a difference in two texts – for example, a similar language feature which has a different effect in the two texts, or how the writers have used language to support their different purposes, appealed to different audiences or created different tones.

Use this skill to help you improve the quality of your writing.

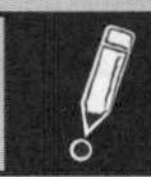

The writer has created a humorous tone in **Source 1**. He has done this by using puns such as ...

However, the writer of **Source 2** has created a much more disturbing tone by ...

Now try this

Look back at the three texts on pages 46 and 47. Choose two of them and answer the exam-style question on the right, using your two chosen texts.

Aim to use the ideas above to help you structure your answer.

4 Compare the different ways in which language is used for effect in the **two** texts. Give some examples and analyse what the effects are. *(16 marks)*

Putting it into practice

In Section A, Question 4 of your exam, you will need to compare the ways language is used for effect in two different source texts. Read Source 1 and Source 2, then look at the question on the next page.

Source 1

We need young people who are able to make a job, not just take a job

by Peter Jones

SOMETHING has gone horribly wrong with our education system. Earlier this year I read a damning report that showed the university dropout rate across Britain had soared. The number of students failing to complete their courses jumped from 28,210 to 31,755 last year – a rise of almost 13%.

But while a university course might be the right option for many young people, increasing numbers of students are realising the benefits of alternative forms of education.

Throughout my career, some of my best hires have been people who have bypassed the traditional route of university and learned their skills through apprenticeship schemes or alternative education courses. They have come to the workplace with a solid understanding of the real world and a steely determination to succeed. Those are the characteristics we need in order to build an entrepreneurial Britain.

For many young people on-the-job training and hands-on experience is the real route to employability, not a university education. Let's give young people the courage and ambition to go for it.

Source 2

CRACKING IDEAS COMPETITION

ENTER THIS YEAR'S COMPLETELY COSMIC CRACKING IDEAS SPACE COMPETITION!

Whether you're into rocket launching science, lunar landscape art, deep space design or galactic gizmo technology this year's Cracking Ideas space competition is just for you. We need your super-sonic, space age Cracking Ideas rocketing their way to us. So ... go on ... go galactic ... get cracking!

HOW TO ENTER YOUR SPACE-AGE IDEAS

Create your cosmic entry:

You can enter this year's Cracking Ideas competition by simply downloading the Moon Bug pack. Or by requesting copies from Cracking Ideas, IPO, FREEPOST CF 4185, Newport, NP20 1ZZ or by emailing ideas@crackingideas.com. You'll be able to construct your special Moon Bug lunar contraption (complete with super-sonic pilots Wallace & Gromit) and then fill in your galactic winning ideas for patents, trade marks, design and copyright.

Alternatively you can use your own materials to make models, take photographs, draw plans or record your cosmic creation in just about any way you feel suits your innovative space-age Cracking Ideas.
All your space-age creations will star in the Cracking Ideas Gallery so keep checking back to see your cosmic entry feature.

Putting it into practice

Look at the exam-style question below and read the extracts from two sample student answers.

Worked example

4 Compare the different ways in which language is used for effect in the two texts.

Give some examples and analyse the effects. *(16 marks)*

Comparing sources

For a question like this you should:

- spend about 20–25 minutes on your answer
- read the sources carefully and note effective use of language
- support points with evidence and a clear explanation focusing on **effect**
- use **connectives** to compare and contrast the two sources.

Sample answer

Source 1 is aimed at adults and Source 2 is aimed at kids. I know this because one is from a newspaper and the other uses lots of bright colours and images. Source 1 uses some persuasive language to make the reader think. For example, he says 'Something has gone horribly wrong with our education system', which makes the reader pay attention.

Source 2 talks directly to the reader to persuade them: 'this year's Cracking Ideas space competition is just for you'.

✗ The task asks you to focus on language, not on presentation.

✓ A reasonable point supported with evidence.

✗ A limited comment on the effect of language.

✗ There is no comment or explanation on how or why direct address is persuasive.

This answer contains misplaced comments on presentation and no clear comparison or contrast.

Improved sample answer

Both texts are persuasive. Source 1 aims to persuade readers that a university degree is not essential for success while Source 2 aims to persuade readers to take part in the Cracking Ideas competition. They both address the reader directly ('you... we') to engage and involve the reader. Source 1 does this to make the reader feel that this issue is relevant to us all, whereas Source 2 wants the reader to feel that this competition is something which they would want to take part in.

✓ Identifies the purpose to focus the answer on the effect of the language used.

✓ Identifies a similarity in language use.

✓ Developed comment on the effect of this language technique.

This answer is focused on the task, establishing purpose and viewpoint. It identifies a similarity in language use and a difference in its effect.

Now try this

Complete the 'Improved sample answer'. Write at least **two** more paragraphs comparing the ways in which language is used for effect in the two texts.

Had a look ☐ Nearly there ☐ Nailed it! ☐

Reading the questions

Before you get stuck into your revision for Section B: Writing, you need to know –

- **how to pick out the key information in the questions**
- how long you have to spend on each answer.

You need to read each question in the exam very carefully to make sure you know exactly what the question is asking you to do. This page will help you practice this.

What the questions tell you

The questions in **Section B: Writing** tell you what you need to know in order to write an effective answer. Look at this example. Don't try to answer the question – just get used to the style.

> **6** Your school or college magazine is inviting students to write an article with the title 'Money isn't everything.' Write an article arguing **either** *for* **or** *against* this point of view. *(24 marks)*

This tells you your **audience** – who you are writing for. It suggests you are writing for students / parents / teachers.

This tells you your **form** – what kind of text you are writing. Here, it is a magazine article.

This tells you the **topic** – what you are writing about. Here, it is the importance of money compared to other things.

This tells you your **purpose** – what your text must achieve. Here, you need to argue your point of view.

What the questions don't tell you

The exam questions will **not** remind you about the assessment objectives being used to assess your writing, so you need to remember what they are.

Communicate clearly, effectively and imaginatively, using and adapting forms and selecting vocabulary appropriate to task and purpose in ways which engage the reader.

For this assessment objective you should:

- express your ideas clearly
- use the right form (letter, newspaper article, etc.)
- choose effective and appropriate vocabulary to keep the reader interested.

Organise information and ideas into structured and sequenced sentences, paragraphs and whole texts, using a variety of linguistic and structural features to support cohesion and overall coherence.

For this assessment objective you should:

- plan and structure your work in sentences and paragraphs
- use connectives and other devices to link your ideas and make them easy to follow.

Use a range of sentence structures for clarity, purpose and effect, with accurate punctuation and spelling.

For this assessment objective you should:

- vary the length and types of sentences you use
- spell and punctuate accurately.

Now try this

Look at this exam-style question.

> **5** A national newspaper is inviting students to write an article called 'Dream School'. Write your article, describing what you think would be the perfect school and explaining why. *(16 marks)*

Don't try to answer this exam question. Instead, note down:

- the audience it is asking you to write for
- the **two** purposes your text should achieve
- the form it is asking you to use
- the topic it is asking you to write about.

The questions and planning your exam time

Before you get stuck into your revision for Section B: Writing, you need to know –

- how to pick out the key information in the questions
- **how many questions are on the paper and how long you have to spend on each answer.**

In Section B, you will be given **two** writing tasks. You must complete **both of them**.

- **Question 5** asks you to complete a piece of writing to **inform, explain or describe**. For example:

> **5** A national newspaper is inviting students to write an article called 'Dream School'. Write your article, describing what you think would be the perfect school and explaining why. *(16 marks)*

> **5** What is the one thing which would make the biggest difference to teenagers' lives? Write an article for a magazine of your choice informing the reader about the 'one thing' you have chosen and explaining why it would make such a difference. *(16 marks)*

> **5** Write an article for your school or college website, informing readers about GCSEs and explaining why they are important. *(16 marks)*

- **Question 6** asks you to complete a piece of writing to **persuade** or **argue** a point of view. For example:

> **6** 'Watching television is a waste of everybody's time.' Write an article for a magazine of your choice which persuades your readers that this statement is **either** *right* **or** *wrong*. *(24 marks)*

> **6** Your school or college magazine is inviting students to write an article with the title 'Money isn't everything.' Write an article arguing **either** *for* **or** *against* this point of view. *(24 marks)*

> **6** Write an article for a travel website, persuading visitors to come and spend some time exploring your local area. *(24 marks)*

How much time to spend on each question?

You have **one hour** to complete both writing tasks. The instructions on the exam paper advise you to:

- spend 25 minutes on **Question 5**, which is worth 16 marks
- spend 35 minutes on **Question 6**, which is worth 24 marks.

So you could organise your time like this:

Question 5: 25 mins		Question 6: 35 mins	
Plan the answer:	5 mins	**Plan** the answer:	5 mins
Write the answer:	17 mins	**Write** the answer:	27 mins
Check the answer:	3 mins	**Check** the answer:	3 mins
	25 mins		35 mins

Now try this

Look at one of the Question 6 exam-style questions above. Don't try to answer it. Instead note down:

- the audience it is asking you to write for
- the purpose your text should achieve
- the form it is asking you to use
- the topic it is asking you to write about.

Writing for an audience

The writing tasks will often tell you the audience you are writing for. You need to make your writing appealing, appropriate and accessible **to that audience**.

Audience

The audience you are writing for may be clearly **stated** in the task:

> Write a guide for Year 7 students informing them about …

In this example, you need to write for an audience of 11–12 year-old school students.

Or the audience may be **implied** in the task:

> Write an article for your school or college magazine in which you …

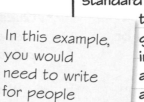

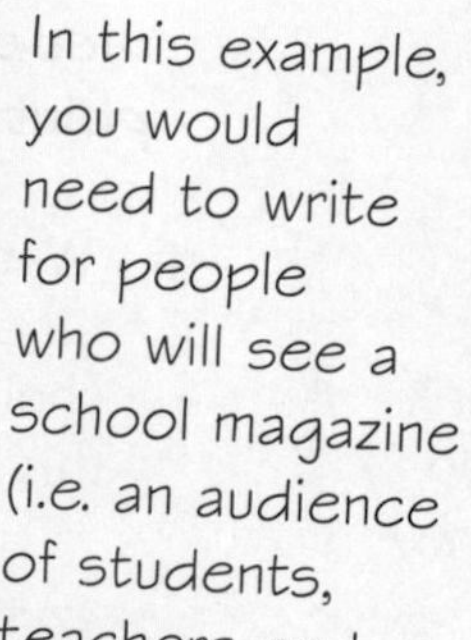
In this example, you would need to write for people who will see a school magazine (i.e. an audience of students, teachers and parents).

Formality and standard English

You will need to use formal language and standard English for most of the writing tasks and audiences you will be given in the exam. (Only use informal language where it is appropriate for the purpose and audience of your writing.) So you should avoid:

- slang (e.g. I was gutted)
- non-standard English (e.g. I haven't never done that)
- abbreviations (e.g. You shouldn't)
- text language (e.g. Ha ha LOL).

Language and audience

You may be asked to write for a teenage audience or for younger children.

> Write a guide for teenagers, explaining how …

If you are asked to write a text for teenagers you may want to include some slang.

If I use some slang, I may make a younger audience feel like I am talking to them in their own language.

If I use too much slang and other informal language, I may make my writing seem careless and unreliable.

If you are writing for an audience of Year 7 students, you should choose appropriate, accessible language like:

> Don't leave homework until the night before it's due in!

rather than:

> It is highly inadvisable to delay the completion of independent study tasks until shortly before the deadline for submission.

Think about your audience's age, and the language they would use and understand.

Worked example

5 Write an article for your school or college website, informing readers about GCSEs and explaining why they are important.

(16 marks)

You reckon you've got ages until your GCSEs. You reckon, so what? But I'm telling you, you're gonna be doing GCSEs before you know it.

You need to start working on them right now!

This answer is far too informal. The text should be appropriate for students and parents – and formal enough to suggest the information is reliable.

Now try this

Rewrite the opening paragraph of the student answer opposite, using formal standard English appropriate to the audience suggested in the task.

Writing for a purpose: inform and explain

When you write with the purpose of informing and explaining, there are a number of techniques you can use. These will help you organise your writing, engage your audience and achieve your purpose.

Techniques to inform and explain

Headings and subheadings

- Use headings to organise texts to help find information.
- Use subheadings to help pick out key areas to include when planning writing.

Structure

Information and explanation texts are usually organised chronologically. To signpost this to the reader use connectives:

- First …
- Then …
- Next …
- Finally …

Facts and statistics

These suggest that the information in a text can be trusted. Use facts and statistics:

- from the source texts in Section A: Reading
- you already know that are relevant to the writing task.

Tone

Aim for a formal tone to suggest to the reader that the information is unbiased and reliable. Use:

- formal language
- Standard English
- third person (he, she, they).

Language

Because information texts are factual and formal avoid using in your writing:

- figurative language
- rhetorical devices.

Facts and statistics are supposed to be believable, for instance, this seems believable: 'Our school recycles nearly 70% of its waste paper' and this less believable 'Our school recently completed a sponsored walk which raised over £1 million for charity.'

EXAM SKILL

You can still use a simile, some alliteration or other language devices – but always stick to the purpose of the text. Don't lose focus and start to persuade or argue when you are supposed to be informing or explaining.

Use this skill to help you improve the quality of your writing.

Now try this

Look at this exam-style question and then complete tasks 1 to 4 opposite:

> **5** Write a guide to appear in a magazine for parents informing them about the difficulties of being a teenager today and explaining how parents can help them.
> *(16 marks)*

1. Write down **five** subheadings you could use to organise your writing.
2. Write a sentence describing the tone you would use in this task, and how you would achieve it.
3. Write down any facts or statistics you could include in your writing.
4. Write the **first two** sentences of your answer.

Had a look ☐ Nearly there ☐ Nailed it! ☐

Writing for a purpose: describe

When you write with the purpose of describing something, there are a number of techniques you can use. These will help you engage your reader and achieve your purpose.

The five senses

When you write to describe a place or an experience, you want the reader to experience what it was like to *be* there.

The only way we can experience anything is through our senses:

Often writers focus on the sense of sight. By using the other four senses as well, you can create **much** more vivid descriptions.

Figurative language

Figurative language, or **imagery**, can create an image in the reader's mind. It includes language devices such as:

- similies
- metaphors
- personification.

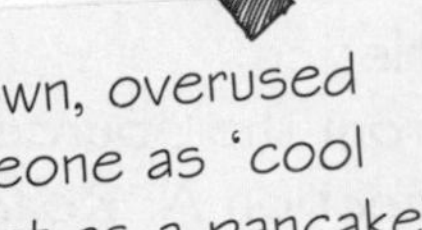

Used sparingly and imaginatively, figurative language can help to create rich and powerful descriptions.

Remember to avoid clichés (well-known, overused figurative language). Describing someone as 'cool as a cucumber' or a landscape as 'flat as a pancake' does **not** demonstrate imagination and originality.

Feelings

Describing the narrator's feelings can bring descriptive writing to life. It helps the reader understand and share those feelings. Remember to **show** the reader how the narrator feels, rather than **tell** them. For example, it is much more effective to write:

 A smile spread across my face and warm satisfaction rose from my stomach to the tips of my ears.

than:

 I felt really, really happy.

Language choice

In descriptive writing, it can be tempting to use as much descriptive language as possible. It's much more effective to use fewer words which you have chosen really carefully. Try to use one precise descriptive word, rather than three vague words. For example:

 I danced across the road

creates a much more immediate and powerful picture than:

✗ I walked cheerfully with a spring in my step across the road as though I were dancing.

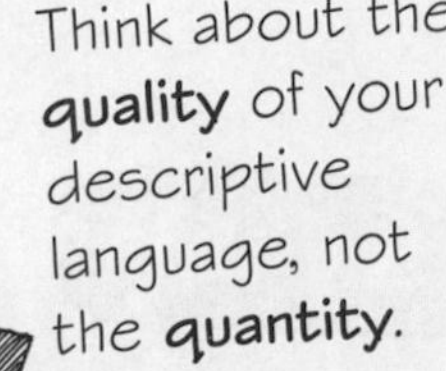

Think about the **quality** of your descriptive language, not the **quantity**.

Now try this

Write the first paragraph of your response to this question.

Describe a time when you were frightened.

You should choose your language for quality, not quantity. In your writing, try to use:

- at least two different senses
- a description of your feelings
- at least one example of figurative language.

Writing for a purpose: argue and persuade

When you write with the purpose of arguing and persuading, there are a number of techniques you can use to help you engage your reader and achieve your purpose.

Key points

The power of your persuasion relies on the strength of your key points. To argue your opinion, choose key points which highlight:

- why you are right
- why those who disagree are wrong.

To persuade your reader, choose key points which highlight:

- what is **wrong** with the way things are
- how your ideas will make things **better**.

Evidence

Always support **each** of your key points with convincing evidence. This could be:

- a fact or statistic
- an expert opinion
- an example from your own experience.

Connectives

Also see page 70

Use connectives to signpost the path your argument is going to follow.

To build your argument, you could use:

- furthermore …
- moreover …
- additionally …

To introduce counter-arguments, you can use:

- however …
- on the other hand …

To explain your argument, you could use:

- consequently …
- therefore …

Counter-arguments

Think about the ways in which your reader might disagree with you – and then point out why they are wrong. This is an effective way of discussing opposing ideas. For example:

Your reader may have different ideas about the way things are or the way to make things better. You can dismiss these ideas using a counter-argument.

Some people firmly believe that teenagers are lazy, aggressive and uncaring. But it is the media who constantly feed us these negative images, while ignoring all those teenagers who work hard, behave responsibly and even raise money for good causes.

Rhetorical devices

These can add great power to your argument.

To engage and influence your reader, you can use:

- rhetorical questions
- direct address.

To add power to your argument, use:

- repetition
- lists
- alliteration
- contrast
- patterns of three
- emotive language
- hyperbole.

Also see pages 33 and 34

Now try this

Note down some ideas which you could use in your response to the question below:

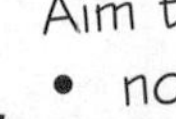

6 Write an article for your school magazine persuading students to enter a talent show you are organising. *(24 marks)*

Aim to:

- note down three key points, supported with evidence
- identify and dismiss a counter-argument
- write three sentences using three different rhetorical devices.

Had a look ☐ Nearly there ☐ Nailed it! ☐

Putting it into practice

Before you start thinking about the writing tasks and how to complete them, work out how long you should spend on each question.

Here is one student's exam plan for Section B: Writing. Now write their planning and checking time as well.

Timing
Q5: 25 mins (10.00–10.25am)

Q6: 35 mins (10.25–11.00am)

Reading the questions

When you first look at **Section B: Writing** you should:

- ✓ plan your time – you have one hour
- ✓ read each question carefully
- ✓ note the task's purpose, audience and form
- ✓ note the key features you need to remember for the text you are going to write.

Look carefully at each question and make sure you identify exactly what the question is asking you to do. Look at how this student has highlighted the key features of this question:

5 A local newspaper is inviting entries for a writing competition, asking writers to write an article describing the most important day of their life so far, and explaining what made it important. Write your entry. *(16 marks)*

Now try this

Look closely at the exam-style question opposite. Pick out the key information about:

- which audience to write for
- the form in which you should write
- the purpose your writing should achieve
- the topic of your writing.

6 The head of your school or college has written a letter to staff, students and parents announcing that the school playing fields are to be sold and the money used to build a new science block and school library. Write a letter to the head, arguing **either** *for* **or** *against* this idea. *(24 marks)*

Form: letters and emails

You may be asked to write a letter or an email for either of the writing tasks in your exam. Show that you know what you are doing by using the key features of the form in which you have been asked to write – and by setting them out correctly.

In formal letters:

- Your address goes in the top right-hand corner.
- Put the date underneath your address.
- The person you are writing to and their address goes on the left, lower down.
- Yours has a capital letter – but **sincerely** and **faithfully** do not.
- Print your name beneath your signature.

17 Jordan Avenue
Brimworth
Brimshire BX17 M3U

17 February 2013

The Editor
Brimshire Gazette
17 High Street
Brimworth
Brimshire
BX1 8TT

Dear Sir/Madam

I am writing to express my concerns at the

and hope that it never happens again.

Yours faithfully

Andrew Aidan

If you use the name of the person you are writing to here, then end with **Yours sincerely**. If you use 'Dear Sir/Madam', then end with **Yours faithfully**. A letter to a friend or relative might end less formally with **Lots of love** or **Cheers**.

Formal emails use some of the same features as formal letters.

- Note that postal addresses and the date are not included in emails.
- Like a formal letter, you begin **Dear** …
- You can end with **Yours sincerely** or with something a little less formal.

Dear Mr Patel
I am writing to apply for the position advertised in the Brimshire Gazette.

I look forward to hearing from you.

Best wishes
Andrew Aidan.

In **inFormal emails:**

- Postal addresses and the date are not included.
- You can begin Hi or Hello …
- You can end with something much less formal.

Hi Annie
Mum told me that you were thinking of doing some volunteer work so I thought I'd write and

Lots of love
Andy

Now try this

Look back at the formal letter-writing task on page 58. List all the key features of a formal letter that you would include in your letter.

Had a look ☐ Nearly there ☐ Nailed it! ☐

Form: articles

You may be asked to write a newspaper, magazine or web article for either of the writing tasks in your exam.

The headline gives enough information to intrigue the reader – and may use a pun, alliteration, repetition, rhetorical question, etc.

The subheading gives more information, drawing the reader in.

The truth about lying: it's the hands that betray you, not the eyes

In the exam, you don't have to write your headline in bold block writing. Your normal handwriting will do.

By analysing videos of liars, the team found there was no link to their eye movements

ADAM SHERWIN

The writer's name, or byline.

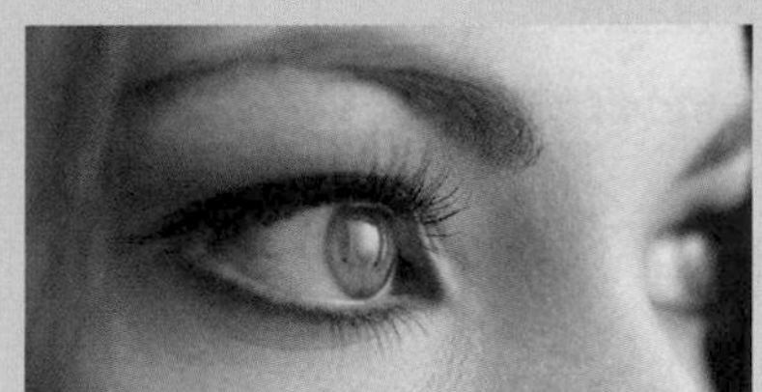

The eyes don't lie.

It is often claimed that even the most stone-faced liar will be betrayed by an unwitting eye movement.

But new research suggests that "lying eyes", which no fibber can avoid revealing, are actually a myth.

Verbal hesitations and excessive hand gestures may prove a better guide to whether a person is telling untruths, according to research conducted by Professor Richard Wiseman.

Many psychologists believe that when a person looks up to their right they are likely to be telling a lie. Glancing up to the left, on the other hand, is said to indicate honesty.

But the experts are wrong, according to Prof Wiseman, a psychologist from the University of Hertfordshire: 'The results of the first study revealed no relationship between lying and eye movements, and the

Opening paragraphs summarise the key points to engage the reader.

Later paragraphs add more detail.

Quotations from experts or people involved in the story add interest and authenticity.

Now try this

Look at this exam-style question.

6 Write an article for your school or college magazine persuading students to enter a talent show you are organising. *(24 marks)*

Write the first **three** paragraphs of your article. Try to:

- sum up your key ideas in paragraph 1
- add more detail in paragraph 2
- use a quotation in paragraph 3.

Form: information sheets

You may be asked to write an information sheet for either of the writing tasks in your exam.

Headings and subheadings

Headings and subheadings can engage the reader's attention. They can also guide the reader through the information available.

Bullet points and numbered lists

Lists can provide a lot of information in a short space. Numbered lists can be used to show ranking, or a chronological sequence of events.

Worked example

5 Produce a leaflet, informing other students about a sport or activity which your school or college offers. *(16 marks)*

Learning the drums

Five great reasons to learn the drums

1

2

3

4

5

Getting started

The first things you will learn are:

-
-
-

Buying a drum kit

You don't need to spend a fortune to learn the drums. Just buy a pair of sticks and a practice pad!

Text boxes can be used to highlight key information. Remember, you can use boxes, tables and charts to present large amounts of information quickly and clearly.

Playing in a band

Now try this

Plan your own response to the exam-style question above. Note down:

- a heading
- **four** or **five** key subheadings
- any text boxes, tables, charts or lists you would include.

Remember that:

- information sheets often use subheadings to organise the text and guide the reader
- letters or articles written to inform the reader usually do not.

Had a look ☐ Nearly there ☐ Nailed it! ☐

Putting it into practice

Look at the exam-style question below and read the two sample student answers.

Worked example

6 Your local council is asking all young people in the area to give up two or three hours a month to do some voluntary work.

Write a letter to your local council arguing **either** *for* **or** *against* this idea. *(24 marks)*

For each writing question you should:

- spend a minute or two reading the question carefully
- note the form, purpose, audience and topic for the task
- check you have included all the key features of the form.

Sample answer

10 High Street
Townville
TO13 2UX

Dear Council

I am writing to tell you that I think it's a really bad idea to ask young people to help out at

So I hope you will bear this in mind.

Yours

Bill Bradshaw

- ✓ Includes own address, correctly positioned.
- ✗ Does not include date, or address of the person he is writing to.
- ✓ Appropriately formal
- ✗ Inappropriately informal

Improved sample answer

27 Elm Avenue
Bradcaster
Brimshire
BX14 7PI

28 March 2013

Ms P Grimley
Brimshire County Council
PO Box 17
Brimforth
Brimshire BX1 1AA

Dear Ms Grimley

I am writing regarding the council's recent decision to

Yours sincerely
Alice Trimm

All the key features of this letter have been included.

- ✓ Own address
- ✓ Date written
- ✓ Address written to
- ✓ Appropriate formal salutation
- ✓ Correct, formal sign-off

EXAM SKILL

Using the key features of a form will not improve your answer as much as focusing on purpose, audience, language, etc., but it will help.

Use this skill to help you improve the quality of your writing.

Now try this

Write the first and last paragraphs to the exam-style question above.

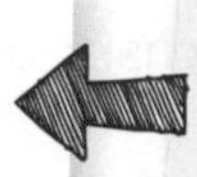

Remember to include all the key features of a formal letter.

Planning an answer: describe

Planning is the only way to produce a well-structured piece of writing, full of relevant, imaginative ideas and carefully crafted language.

Describing a scene

Describe a primary school at the start of a day.

For a question like this, picture the scene in your mind. Divide the scene into sections, then ask yourself:

- What is nearest to you?
- What is beyond that?
- What's in the distance?
- What's furthest from you?

Use the answers to these questions to structure three or four paragraphs:

Plan
1 Parents waving, driving away.
2 Iron gates, playground, hopscotch.
3 School buildings, teacher at window.
4 Clouds gathering, rain coming.

Describing an event

Describe a time when you changed your plans.

You can describe this event in chronological order:

Plan
1 Woke up – excited – day out with Ryan.
2 Ryan rings – dumped me.
3 Sulking. Phone rings. Best friend wants me to go on holiday with her.

OR you can start with a dramatic moment and fill in the gaps later:

Plan
1 Ryan rings – dumped me.
2 Flashback – woke up excited – day out with Ryan.
3 Sulking. Phone rings. Best friend wants me to go on holiday with her.

Gathering ideas

When you've got the basic structure of your piece organised, think about how you can add to your plan using:

- the five senses
- your feelings
- details to create mood or atmosphere
- language for effect.

Plan

1 Parents waving / driving away. Sound of chatter, engines, smell of exhaust

2 Iron gates cold grey, playground, hopscotch – screams / laughter of kids, one crying

3 School buildings, teacher at window building has blank windows like dead eyes; teacher has angry, narrow eyes, menacing

4 Clouds gather, rain coming thunder rumbles, kids scatter like litter on the wind, playground empty, bell rings

Now try this

Choose one of the writing tasks at the top of this page. Plan **four** or **five** paragraphs using your own ideas. Create a mind map or spidergram to bring all your ideas together.

Remember:
- you only have **25 minutes** to plan, write and check this task – so aim for **three** or **four** paragraphs of well-crafted writing
- quality is rewarded – quantity is not
- descriptions needn't be action-packed.

Planning an answer: inform or explain

Familiarise yourself with how to compile a plan so that you will not find it a problem in the exam.

Informing or explaining, or both

Worked example

5 Write a letter to your local council informing them about the facilities for teenagers in your local area and explaining how they could be improved. *(16 marks)*

Plan an introduction that tells your reader what are you writing and why they should read it.

Gather key points to help you organise your ideas. Number your subheadings or key points, putting them in a logical order.

You might want to change your order once you have written your plan.

Add ideas to develop your subheadings or key points. You may decide to combine two key points in one paragraph or divide one key point into two paragraphs.

Sample answer

<u>Plan</u>

Intro
- Not enough facilities.
- Need to improve them.
- Stop teenagers causing problems in town.

2 What do teenagers do?
- Hang around town.
- A few cause trouble.
- Crowds of teens can be intimidating.

1 What is there to do?
- Youth club once a week.
- Cinema / bowling alley but both expensive and both 5 miles away.

3 What can be done?
- Youth club open two or three nights a week.
- Volunteers to do it up.
- Develop waste ground next to station – skate park.
- Teen council to get ideas / suggestions.

Now try this

Look at this exam-style question:

5 What is the one thing which would make the biggest difference to teenagers' lives?

Write an article for a magazine of your choice explaining what the 'one thing' is and why it would make such a difference. *(16 marks)*

Plan your answer, creating a list, mind map or spidergram to bring all your ideas together. Aim to plan **three** or **four** paragraphs.

EXAM SKILL

Remember, even though you will not always include subheadings when you write an information or explanation text, you can still use them to help you plan your writing.

Use this skill to help you improve the quality of your writing.

Planning an answer: argue or persuade

Planning an answer is the only way to produce a well-structured piece of writing, full of relevant, imaginative ideas and carefully crafted language. It is particularly important when writing to plan your argument so it is logically constructed.

Worked example

6 'Watching television is a waste of everybody's time.' Write an article for a magazine of your choice which persuades your readers that this statement is **either** *right* **or** *wrong*. *(24 marks)*

If the question gives you a choice, decide whether you are **for** or **against**. Remember to give your writing a title that reflects your point of view.

Write your introduction, telling the reader what the situation is at the moment, and why that is a problem they need to think about.

Add some evidence to support each key point you make. **Plan key points** by gathering together all the different ideas you can think of that support your viewpoint.

Choose and sequence the most persuasive points. You will probably only need two or three key points.

Don't stop when you've thought of three ideas. Think of more, reject weaker ideas, then put the strong ideas in a logical order.

Add a counter-argument that gives an opposing viewpoint. Then say why you disagree.

Plan a conclusion – your final point to hammer home your argument.

Sample answer

Plan: TV is stealing your life

Intro

100's of channels run all day and all night

Average person watches 4 hours a day – a quarter of their waking life!

2 TV is passive not active

Evidence: my sister – hours spent staring, doing nothing.

Overweight and silent, TV is killing her brain and body.

3 TV is addictive

Once you start, it's difficult to turn off.

Evidence: watch least worst programme, not choosing what to watch.

Don't be afraid to cross out some of your ideas.

~~Advertising is annoying~~

~~10/15 mins of it every hour – they want my money!~~

1 Families don't talk anymore

Evidence: Mine eats dinner in silence in front of the telly.

4 Some say it's educational and entertaining

It can be both – but how often? More often it's neither – e.g. Big Brother.

Conclusion

Most telly is a waste of time for everyone.

Choose what you want to watch – then turn it off.

Now try this

Write a plan for the **other** side of the argument, arguing that television is **not** a waste of time.

Beginnings

Starting a piece of writing can be difficult. Know what you want to write, or you will be in danger of writing one or two boring paragraphs before you really get going.

An effective opening

Your first paragraph of any writing task – and your first sentence in particular – needs to grab the reader's interest and attention. You could use one or more of these five ideas.

- A bold and / or controversial statement:

> Experimenting on animals is a cruel necessity.

- A relevant quotation:

> 'What's in a name? That which we call a rose by any other name would smell as sweet.'
> (William Shakespeare, ***Romeo and Juliet***, 2.2)

- A shocking or surprising fact or statistic:

> 99 per cent of the species that have ever lived on Planet Earth are now extinct.

- A rhetorical question:

> How many of us can honestly say that we care more about others than we do about ourselves?

- A short, relevant, **interesting** anecdote:

> When I was seven, my parents bought me a dog. This was when I first realised that …

EXAM SKILL

Avoid telling the reader what you are going to write about:
In this essay I am going to argue that television is not a waste of time.
Just write it:
Television is informative, educational and interesting.

Use this skill to help you improve the quality of your writing. 

Introducing your topic

After your opening sentence, go on to introduce what you are writing about.

Sample answer

… The average person spends a quarter of their waking life watching television. Are they making good use of their time? Or is television sucking the life out of them, killing them slowly with its mind-numbing mediocrity?

A surprising statistic shocks the reader and grabs their attention. Here, it invites the reader to compare how long they spend watching TV.

Two questions engage the reader, and present the two sides of the argument. The second question makes it clear which side the writer is on.

Now try this

Look at this exam-style question:

> **6** 'There is more to school than passing exams.' Write an article for a magazine of your choice which persuades your readers that this statement is **either** *right* **or** *wrong*. *(24 marks)*

1. Write **three** possible opening sentences that would grab the reader's attention from the start.
2. Choose the best one then complete your introduction, explaining what you are writing about.

Endings

Plan your conclusion before you start writing. The final paragraph of your writing should leave your reader with a lasting impression.

Summing up

Plan your conclusion before you start writing. The final paragraph or conclusion to a text can be used to sum up your ideas – but avoid repeating them. Instead, aim to sum up and emphasise your central idea. You could use one or more of these things.

Avoid introducing your conclusion with phrases like:
- In conclusion ...
- To summarise ...

End on a vivid image: a picture that lingers in the reader's mind. A homeless person sits cold and alone in a shop doorway. As you pass by, you look into her eyes. She can't be older than 15.	**End on a warning:** what will happen if your ideas are not acted on? Within 50 years, the world will have changed beyond all recognition – and our children will blame us for what has happened.	**End on a happy note:** emphasise how great things will be if your ideas are acted on. Ours could be the generation that made the difference.
End on a thought-provoking question: leave the reader thinking. For how long can we ignore what is staring us in the face?	**Refer back to your introduction**, but don't repeat it. I still have that dog – and he's still incredibly badly behaved. But if I hadn't ...	**End on a call to action:** make it clear what you want the reader to do. Don't just sit there. Get up, get out and make it happen.

Worked example

6 'Watching television is a waste of everybody's time.' Write an article for a magazine of your choice which persuades your readers that this statement is **either** *right* **or** *wrong*. *(24 marks)*

How many hours of television have you watched this week? What else could you have done with those hours? Television has turned us all into spectators - and while we're glued to the box, our lives are ticking away, wasted and unused. It's time to stop watching. It's time to start taking part.

Remember that questions engage the reader with the issue – how does it relate to their own life?

A warning.

A final, powerful call to action.

Now try this

Look at the exam-style question opposite.

Choose **one or more** of the above techniques to write a powerful conclusion.

6 'There is more to school than passing exams.' Write an article for a magazine of your choice which persuades your readers that this statement is **either** *right* **or** *wrong*. *(24 marks)*

Putting it into practice

Look at the exam-style question below and read the two sample student plans.

Worked example

5 Write an article for a travel website, describing a place of interest in your area and explaining why visitors would enjoy it.

(16 marks)

Planning

For each writing question you should:

- spend 3–5 minutes gathering ideas
- organise and sequence your ideas
- think about how you will introduce and conclude your writing.

Sample answer

Bradcaster Park

- Good, fun, interesting.
- Playground for kids.
- Lake
-

✗ Some language ideas but undeveloped / unambitious.

✗ Some ideas gathered, but more needed.

Make sure you provide a range of details for questions like this. In this plan there is no detail added about the lake, the information about the park is not sequenced, and there is no introduction or conclusion.

Sample answer

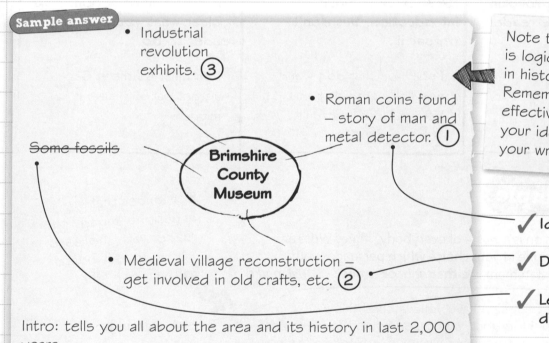

Brimshire County Museum

- Industrial revolution exhibits. (3)
- Roman coins found – story of man and metal detector. (1)
- ~~Some fossils~~
- Medieval village reconstruction – get involved in old crafts, etc. (2)

Intro: tells you all about the area and its history in last 2,000 years.

Conclusion: what life was really like here over the centuries.

Note that the answer is logically sequenced in historical order. Remember that effectively sequencing your ideas will improve your writing.

✓ Ideas gathered.

✓ Detail added.

✓ Less detailed idea discarded.

Now try this

Plan your answer to the above exam-style question and write an opening paragraph.

Remember to:

- gather, organise and sequence your ideas
- plan your introduction and conclusion.

Paragraphing

The best answers are organised into paragraphs. They help structure your writing, making it easier for the reader to follow your thinking and absorb your ideas.

Paragraphs

Use paragraphs to divide your writing into clear points. Paragraphs help the reader follow your ideas and make the whole text more accessible.

one paragraph = one point

Planning can help you paragraph your writing. Make a clear plan, setting out all the points you want to make. Each time you start a new point, start a new paragraph.

Paragraphing for effect

In most cases you should start a new paragraph each time you start a new point. However, you can use shorter paragraphs for effect: to emphasise a point or create a dramatic pause.

News articles often use short paragraphs of just one or two sentences. This creates a sense of pace and keeps the reader 'moving' through the text.

Some people argue there is no clear proof that global warming is a direct result of man's activities. They argue that global warming is a natural cycle which we can do nothing about. They argue that we should do nothing.

This is the road to global disaster.

Doing nothing is precisely what created the problem in the first place. While we sit and wait and see what happens, time is running out.

Structuring paragraphs: argue and persuade

Use Point-Evidence-Explain to structure paragraphs in a piece of writing to argue or persuade.

- A short, clear **point**.
- **Evidence** to support the point.
- **Explains** how the point and evidence are relevant to the main idea.

Britain's weather is changing. Barely a month goes by without it being declared the wettest, the driest, the hottest, the coldest, or the windiest month on record. Our weather is clearly becoming more extreme, and is likely to become even more so. How long can we ignore this before we act?

Structuring paragraphs: inform, explain, describe

Start each paragraph with a **topic sentence** – a sentence that clearly introduces the reader to the content of this paragraph. Use the remainder of the paragraph to develop and add detail to the topic sentence.

- Topic sentence
- Detail / development

Our school has made a huge effort to recycle its waste. Every classroom has a bin just for waste paper which is collected each week by student volunteers. In the canteen, we sort our rubbish into plastics, tin cans, and food waste. Even the staff room has three different bins so teachers can recycle!

Now try this

Write the next paragraph to either of the student answers above.

Had a look ☐ Nearly there ☐ Nailed it! ☐

Using connectives

Connectives help to guide the reader through your ideas. They work like signposts, showing the reader the direction your ideas are taking. They can be used in a variety of ways to improve your writing.

Adding an idea

- Moreover ...
- Furthermore ...
- In addition ...
- Not only ... but also

This will not solve the situation. **Moreover**, it could make it worse.

Not only is this likely to interrupt students' learning, **but also** adds to their stress levels.

Explaining

- Because
- Therefore
- Consequently

Science suggests that the teenage brain needs more sleep to help it grow and develop. **Consequently**, we spend longer in bed.

Teenagers' attitudes and actions are constantly challenged. It is **therefore** unsurprising that they sometimes challenge those who challenge them.

Illustrating

- For example
- For instance
- Such as

Problems, such as vandalism and graffiti and, continue to grow.

Emphasising

- In particular
- Especially
- Significantly

Significantly, these problems increased when the youth club was shut down.

Comparing

- Similarly
- In the same way

It has been argued that an animal's life is not as important as that of a human being. **Similarly**, it has been argued that animals should be exploited for our food, health and wealth.

Contrasting

- However
- On the other hand
- ... whereas ...

Some young people are strongly and unthinkingly influenced by the role models which the media provides. **However**, many are not.

When using a contrasting connective, it's often a good idea to start a new paragraph.

Now try this

Look at the exam-style question opposite. Write as many sentences as you can on this topic, using a different connective in each one.

5 Choose a topic you know a lot about – for example, a hobby, a sport, a person, etc. Write a guide informing the reader about your topic. *(16 marks)*

Putting it into practice

Look at the exam-style question below and read the two sample student answers.

Worked example

6 Your local newspaper is running a campaign to encourage older people to learn about and use computers. Write an article for the newspaper persuading the elderly to discover more about computers and their many benefits. *(24 marks)*

Paragraphing and connectives

For each writing question you should:

- ✓ write in paragraphs
- ✓ plan one point per paragraph
- ✓ use connectives to guide your reader through the text.

Sample answer

One of the most popular things you can do on the internet is social networking. You can go on websites like Facebook and keep in touch with all your friends. You can also use online encyclopedias to find out about anything you want to know. You can also use the internet to save your photos and share them with your friends and relatives on websites like Facebook, which links back to what I was saying before.

✓ A clear point supported with evidence.

✗ This evidence should be supported with a persuasive explanation.

✗ This point should have been sequenced to develop the first point, using a connective to guide the reader.

Remember that a new point should mean a new paragraph. Remember also to support your points with evidence or an explanation. This point contains neither.

Improved sample answer

The internet is a modern miracle: a world of information at your fingertips, waiting to be discovered. Thanks to clever websites called 'search engines', all you have to do is type in a few words and up will pop an enormous choice of websites, all ready to tell you what you want to know. It's so simple, you'll be surfing the internet before you know it.

There are hundreds of things you can do on a computer as well as accessing the internet. For example, you can email friends and relations around the world, sharing your news and views in just a few clicks. It's much quicker than writing a letter – and you don't have to pay a fortune for a stamp, so it can even save you money.

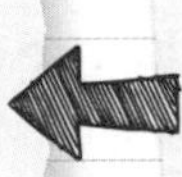

✓ Paragraph clearly organised using:

- point
- evidence
- explanation.

Note here the accurate paragraphing, with links back to the previous paragraph. Note also a connective phrase (For example) to introduce evidence.

Now try this

Write the **first two** or **three** paragraphs of your own answer to the exam-style question above. You could develop some of the ideas from the sample answers, e.g. sharing photos, online encylopedias or social networking.

EXAM SKILL

Remember:

- write in paragraphs
- use Point-Evidence-Explain to structure each paragraph
- use connectives to guide your reader through your ideas.

Use this skill to help you improve the quality of your writing.

Had a look ☐ Nearly there ☐ Nailed it! ☐

Getting the right tone

You need to match your language choice and style to the writing task and its audience.

Formal or informal

Most tasks in the Writing section of your exam will require a formal tone, using standard English and formal language choices. Although some tasks may allow a degree of informality – for example, a task aimed at teenagers – beware of using humour. Ask yourself these questions.

- Is it in keeping with the tone of the rest of my writing?
- Does it add to the impact I want to have on the reader?

Have an audience and form in mind

Most tasks will tell you the audience you are writing for, and the form in which you are writing. If it doesn't, choose a specific form and audience. For example, if you are asked to write to a relative, have a real relative in mind as you write. If you are asked to write for a 'magazine of your own choice', have a particular magazine in mind as you write.

Whatever the writing task, aim to keep your audience and form in mind throughout.

Point of view

Before you start writing, decide whether you will write in the first person (*I*) or third person (*he*, *she*, *they*). **Writing in the third person** gives your writing authority. It suggests to the reader that the writer's opinion is objective and trustworthy.

Writing in the first person can create a relationship between reader and writer. Use it when writing about a personal experience.

Consistent tenses

You are likely to be writing in either the past or present tense in both writing tasks. Whichever tense you start in, make sure you stick to it throughout.

EXAM SKILL

Don't change tense midway through a piece of writing, as it is disconcerting for the reader – and it's a sign that you are not in full control of your writing.

Use this skill to help you improve the quality of your writing.

Worked example

6 'Celebrities have too much influence on our lives.' Write an article for your school or college magazine which persuades your readers that this statement is **either** *right* **or** *wrong*. *(24 marks)*

Celebrities have an extraordinary amount of power and influence in our society. I remember once my mate went totally bananas when she heard that her fave singer was opening a shop near where we live. How mental is that? She thought it was like the most important person in the world doing the most amazing thing in the world.

✓ Formal tone, standard English

✗ Sudden and surprising shift into the first person, informal tone.

✗ Informal language / slang.

Note how the language becomes less formal in tone. This is inconsistent with the first sentence.

Now try this

Rewrite the 'Sample answer' above, aiming to make the tone more consistent and appropriate throughout.

Remember to have your audience firmly in mind to help you keep a consistent and appropriate tone.

Synonyms

Synonyms are words with similar meanings. Use them to avoid repetition and add variety to your writing.

Using synonyms can make your writing more varied and interesting. Having a range of synonyms for key words and ideas in mind as you write will mean that:

- you don't repeat the same key word throughout your writing
- you can pick the most precise word – the one that really says what you want it to say.

Be your own thesaurus

You know hundreds – perhaps thousands – of words that you rarely use. So you don't need a thesaurus to come up with ambitious, effective vocabulary chosen for its impact. You just need to think through your mental thesaurus. Beware though! Don't use a word if you are not absolutely sure of its precise meaning.

Examples of synonyms

Comments on evidence often involve the phrase This suggests ... Replace it with:

- This gives the impression that ...
- It seems clear that ...
- This implies ...
- In other words ...

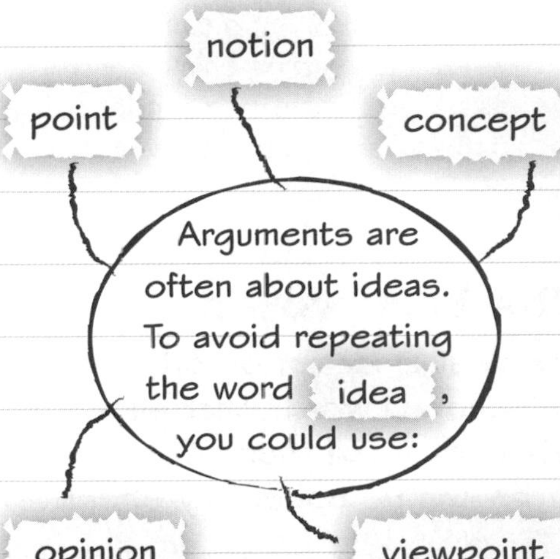

Worked example

6 'Celebrities have too much influence on our lives.' Write an article for your school or college magazine which persuades your readers that this statement is **either** *right* **or** *wrong*. *(24 marks)*

The idea of celebrities as perfect role models is not the only misguided idea connected with the world of the celebrity. Some people have the idea that celebrities should be consulted on everything from international politics to haircare.

EXAM SKILL

Using the same word more than once can undo all the hard word you put into an answer, making your ideas seem repetitive and uninteresting.

Use this skill to help you improve the quality of your writing.

Repetition can add pace and rhythm to your writing – but there are too many words being repeated too often here, weakening an otherwise strong paragraph.

Now try this

Rewrite the 'Sample answer' above, replacing the words 'celebrities', 'celebrity' and 'idea' with different synonyms.

Before you start, make a list of all the synonyms you can think of for the word 'celebrity'. You can use a thesaurus if you get stuck.

Choosing vocabulary for effect: describe

Choosing the most effective vocabulary can have a significant impact on your writing, especially when you are writing to **describe**.

Don't overdo it

When writing to describe, it is important that you do just that. However, be careful not to overdo it. Avoid piling on the adjectives and adverbs:

✗ The sun's glorious golden rays burst through my gleaming windows, sending shimmering sparkling beams of incandescence dancing around my walls.

Describe what matters – not what doesn't

Don't describe everything. Focus on what matters. For example, if you want to describe a phone call shattering an awkward silence, focus on the relevant detail:

✗ The insistent ringtone of the phone suddenly filled the room so I hurried to the low, wooden table on which it sat and picked up the slim black handset, pressing it to my ear.

✓ The jangling phone made me jump. I answered it.

The best words

The best description often uses fewer, well-chosen words that **show** the reader, rather than **tell** them. Carefully chosen verbs can be especially effective:

✗ He walked across the room with a spring in his step. → ✓ He bounced across the room.

✗ He flung open the door and walked quickly into the room. → ✓ He flew into the room.

However, sometimes showing the reader takes more words than telling them. Here are a couple of rules.

Don't name your feelings:

✗ I felt really really terrified.

✓ I clenched my clammy palms into fists and tried to stop my legs shaking.

Do describe the effect they have on you:

✗ It hurt a lot.

✓ Pain shot through me like a thunderbolt.

Describing people

Choose just one or two details that will give the reader an impression of a person. For example, two of the details opposite could be used to show the reader that this person is concerned about their appearance. The others tell you very little.

✗ Brown hair
✗ Brown eyes
✗ Glasses
✗ Dark trousers

✓ Wearing a tie
✓ Highly polished shoes

Now try this

Write the opening paragraph of the question below, describing your feelings as you come face-to-face with your fear.

Describe a time when you faced a fear.

Remember:

- your task is to describe, **not** to tell a story, so focus on describing the situation, your thoughts and feelings
- choose only relevant details to describe
- choose the best words that show the reader how you felt.

Choosing vocabulary for effect: argue and persuade

When writing to argue or persuade, you need to be able to use a wide vocabulary of emotive words and positive and negative language.

Vocabulary for impact

Using emotive language can add impact to your argument. For example, you may think that global warming is a problem. To shock your reader into action, you want to emphasise the problem by choosing a more emotive word:

If we ignore global warming now, we will soon be facing a ~~problem~~

catastrophe | disaster | calamity

Add even more power to your sentence by intensifying the emotive word:

horrific | alarming | terrifying

we will soon be facing a terrifying catastrophe.

Positive and negative

If you frame your ideas in **positive** or **negative** language you can control your reader's reaction to them. For example,

If you **support** fox hunting, it could be described as: 'A humane method of pest control.'

If you **oppose** fox hunting, it could be described as: 'A cruel and barbaric sport.'

If you are arguing in **support** of typical teenage behaviour, you could point out that: 'Sleep is an essential ingredient for the teenage brain's development.'

Taking the **opposing point of view** you might write: 'Idle teenagers lounge in bed for hours, paralysed by their crippling laziness.'

Connotations

You can guide your reader's reaction by thinking about the connotations of your vocabulary choice. Look at these words. Each one has a similar meaning but carries different associations.

Six hours of intensive revision can make you [ ]

- exhausted. — extreme, intense
- drained. — implies weak, empty
- sleepy. — sounds childish, mocking

Fox hunting is [ ]

- brutal. — emphasises violence
- barbaric. — suggests uncivilised
- heartless. — emphasises lack of feeling or empathy

Now try this

Write an opening paragraph for the exam-style question opposite, focusing on vocabulary to persuade the reader.

6 'School is cruel.' Write an article for a magazine of your choice which persuades your readers that this statement is **either** *right* **or** *wrong*. *(24 marks)*

Remember to choose vocabulary for its impact and for its connotations.

Had a look ☐ Nearly there ☐ Nailed it! ☐

Language for effect 1

You can use a range of language techniques to add power and impact to your writing.

Rhetorical questions

Use these in argument or persuasive writing to lead the reader to the answer you want.

There is really only one way to answer these questions:

> Who in their right mind would do such a thing?

> Would you stand by and do nothing if you saw a human being treated like this?

You can also use them in descriptive writing to engage the reader in a situation:

> What was going on?

> What should I do?

Contrast

Place two opposing ideas or situations in direct contrast to emphasise the difference.

> You can work hard in a job you hate for the rest of your life

> or you can work hard on your GCSEs for a couple of years and get the job you want.

You can also use contrast in descriptive writing to exaggerate a detail: 'Among all the smiling, happy faces there was just one exception: my father's sour-faced, snarling scowl.'

Repetition

Repeating a word or phrase can emphasise a key point or idea in an argument:

> Chasing a helpless animal across open country is cruel. Setting a pack of dogs on a helpless animal is cruel. Watching as the dogs butcher the helpless animal is cruel.

It can also add emphasis to an idea in descriptive writing:

> There is no point in discussing it, there is no point in arguing about it, there is no point in shouting about it. Once my father has made up his mind, it is made up.

Lists

Use a list to suggest a range of ideas in your persuasive writing:

> It's quick, simple, easy and cheap.

> The improvement would be huge: students would learn more, learn faster, be more motivated, enjoy school more and achieve better results.

Use it to suggest range or variety in your descriptive writing.

> Scattered across the carpet were balloons, paper hats, lumps of cake, streamers and torn shreds of wrapping paper.

Now try this

Choose **one** of these questions:

1. Describe your favourite place.
2. **6** Write an article for your school or college magazine persuading students to take more exercise and lead a healthier life. *(24 marks)*

Write **four** short extracts from your chosen task, using **one** of the language techniques above in each.

EXAM SKILL

Don't use these language devices as a tick list in the exam, aiming to include one of each in both of your answers.

Instead, look for opportunities where they will add to the impact of your ideas.

Use this skill to help you improve the quality of your writing.

Language for effect 2

You can use a range of language techniques to add power and impact to your writing.

Direct address

Talking directly to the reader is persuasive. Using the **second person 'you'** can suggest that your ideas are relevant to their lives. For example:

'**you** can get involved in lots of different ways'

this involves the reader and is much more persuasive than:

'There are many ways to get involved.'

Using the **first person plural 'we'** can create a relationship between you, the writer, and the reader. It suggests that we are all in the same situation, facing the same problems:

'If **we** do nothing, then nothing will change. It is up to us to act and act now.'

Pattern of three

Putting words or phrases in linked groups of three adds rhythm and emphasis to your ideas in all kinds of writing:

It doesn't matter if you're a beginner, an improver, or an expert. It's fun for everyone!

It will benefit the students, the teachers, and the community as a whole.

I approached the front door. My hands were cold, clammy and shaking.

Alliteration

Alliteration can add rhythm and emphasis to your writing. Remember: the alliterative words do not have to be next to each other – just near each other.

It was a truly terrifying experience.

Combined with other language techniques, alliteration can be particularly engaging and powerful: 'It's fun, fast and furious.'

Hyperbole

Exaggeration can:

- add humour to an argument or a description:

The house looked like a herd of elephants had run through it, detonating hand grenades as they went.

- emphasise a key point:

Teachers want their students to sit completely still and in total silence for six hours a day.

Now try this

Choose **one** of these questions:

1 Describe a time when you felt under pressure.

2 **6** 'Mobile phones are killing young people's ability to communicate.' Write a letter to your local paper, arguing **either** *for* **or** *against* this point of view. *(24 marks)*

Write **four** short extracts from your chosen task, using **one** of the language techniques above in each.

Had a look ☐ Nearly there ☐ Nailed it! ☐

Language for effect 3

You can use figurative language to create a powerful image in your readers' minds. Used carefully and sparingly, they can also demonstrate imagination, originality and writing craftsmanship. This page explains three types of figurative language: similes, metaphor and personification.

Similes

A simile is a comparison, usually using **as** or **like**, suggesting a resemblance between one thing and another. It can be used when writing:

- **to inform**

> When you get it right, skateboarding can be as exhilarating as a skydive from 30,000 feet.

- **to persuade**

> Smoking cigarettes is like a game of Russian roulette – and the chances are, you'll end up losing.

Personification

Personification is the technique of describing something non-human as if it were human. It can be used when writing:

- **to describe**

> Sunlight danced on the water as we headed out to sea.

- **to persuade**

> Smoking is highly addictive and, once the habit has got its hands around your throat, it will not let go.

Metaphor

A metaphor is a direct comparison suggesting a resemblance between one thing and another. It can be used when writing:

- **to argue**

> At night, when there is nothing else to do, the youth club is a bright light in the darkness, drawing all the young people of the town through its doors.

- **to describe**

> She stared and stared, her eyes burning holes in my face.

Avoiding clichés

While an imaginative and original simile or metaphor can add greatly to your writing, a cliché can destroy the effect. So no matter how hurried you are, **do not** describe someone as:

- cool as a cucumber
- white as a sheet
- blind as a bat

... or any other comparison that your reader will have read hundreds of times before.

Now try this

Choose **one** of these questions:

1. Describe your ideal home.
2. 6 'Young people grow up too fast. We should let children be children for as long as possible.' Write an article for a magazine of your choice, arguing **either** *for* **or** *against* this point of view. *(24 marks)*

Write **three** short extracts from your chosen task, using **one** of the language techniques above in each.

EXAM SKILL

Remember these dos and don'ts.

- Don't try to use one simile, one metaphor and one personification in both of your answers.
- Do look for opportunities where they will add to the impact of your ideas.
- Do avoid clichés and be original.

Use this skill to help you improve the quality of your writing.

Putting it into practice

Look at the exam-style question below and read the two sample student answers.

Worked example

5 Describe a time when you made a mistake and explain what the consequences were. Your writing will appear in the *Life and Times* section of your local newspaper. *(16 marks)*

Language choice

In each of your writing tasks you should:

- ✓ choose language appropriate to your audience
- ✓ make ambitious and effective vocabulary choices to engage your reader
- ✓ use a range of language techniques.

Sample answer

The worst mistake I ever made was jumping out of a tree. I was down the park with my friends and they dared me to climb this really tall tree. I was about eight. So I climbed up the tree. I got about a metre up and it felt like I was nearly at the sky. I looked down and realised I hadn't got very far and they were all laughing and shouting and encouraging me to go higher. So I carried on climbing. I went up another metre or so. By now I was really scared.

✗ Language choice too informal for this audience.

✗ Limited description, and unambitious vocabulary choice.

✓ Effective use of figurative language.

Note that although there is some limited (but effective) language choice here, there are also missed opportunities to use really effective language (as you can see in the final sentence).

Improved sample answer

My aunt had come to stay. She was a stern, grey-faced woman with eyes that could turn you to stone. When she entered a room, an arctic cold crept through the air, freezing you instantly into silence. The only thing that would make my aunt crack her face and bring out a smile was cake. She loved it. Cream cake, chocolate cake, fruit cake, any cake would bring a rosy glow to her cheeks and her long, sharpened teeth out from between her grey lips. And that was where the trouble started.

✓ Engaging vocabulary choice.

✓ Effective use of language devices:

- metaphor
- personification
- list.

Notice how this language choice shows humour as well as being effective.

Now try this

Write the **first two** paragraphs of your answer to the exam-style question above.

Remember to choose and use:

- language appropriate to your audience
- language for effect
- a range of ambitious vocabulary and language features.

Sentence variety 1

Using a range of different sentence types adds variety to your writing and helps keep your readers engaged.

Adding variety

Writing for young children uses a limited range of sentence types:

> Penny went out of the house.
> It was raining.
> Soon she was soaked.
> Penny turned around and went home again.

Effective writing for adults uses a variety of sentence types to hold the reader's interest.

Sentence types

There are four basic types of sentence:

- ✓ simple
- ✓ compound
- ✓ complex
- ✓ minor.

To remind yourself which is which, look back at page 36. You should use all four in your writing for variety and for effect.

Complex sentences

Complex sentences give you the most opportunity to achieve variety. There are two main types.

1 Sentences using a subordinating clause

- This is additional information which is added to the main clause using connectives such as: because, although, after, if, since.
- The subordinate clause is dependent on the main clause because it doesn't make sense without it.

Subordinating clause / **Main clause**

> Before I went out, I locked all the doors.

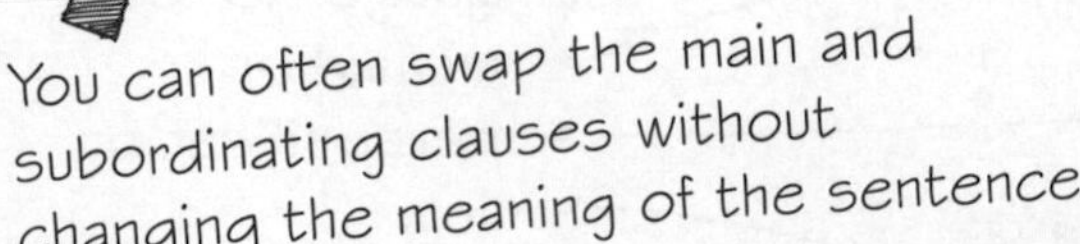

You can often swap the main and subordinating clauses without changing the meaning of the sentence.

2 Sentences using a relative clause

This is where additional information is introduced use a **relative pronoun**, such as: that, where, which, whose, who, when.

Main clause / **Relative clause, separated from the main clause with commas**

> The neighbour, who I've never liked, waved as I walked down the front path.

Main clause / **Relative clause, separated from the main clause with commas**

> The last time I saw him, which was over a week ago, had ended in disaster.

Now try this

Write the opening paragraph for this question:

> Describe a place you know well. It could be a room in your house, a street, a town, or somewhere you have visited.

Aim to use at least one of each sentence type:

- a simple sentence
- a compound sentence
- a complex sentence with a subordinating clause
- a complex sentence with a relative clause
- a minor sentence.

Sentence variety 2

Thinking about the first word of your sentences can help you add interest to your writing.

First words

Developing writers often start their sentences in similar ways. Try to start your sentences in different ways to add variety to your writing. You can start with any of these.

Type of word	Examples
A pronoun I, you, he, she, it, we, they, my, your	I turned and started.
An article a, an, the	The glass had disappeared.
A preposition above, behind, between, near, with, etc.	Above me, I heard footsteps.
An -ing word (or present participle) running, hurrying, crawling, smiling, etc.	Edging silently to the door, I went to the stairs and listened.
An adjective slow, quiet, huge, violent, etc.	Sharp, prickling pains crept from my fingertips to my hair.
An adverb alarmingly, painfully, happily, etc.	Gingerly, I put my foot on the first stair.
A connective (subordinating clause + main clause) if, although, because, etc.	Although I knew I was in an empty house, I could not help thinking that I was not alone.

Now try this

Write the **first ten** sentences for the question below:

Describe your most memorable moment at school.

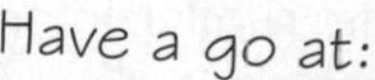

Have a go at:
- using all seven different types of sentence opener in your writing
- using a different word to start each of your sentences.

Had a look ☐ Nearly there ☐ Nailed it! ☐

Sentences for effect

Structuring your sentences in different ways can achieve different effects. Practise using various sentence structures to emphasise your argument.

Longer sentences

Use longer sentences to deliver more information sharply and concisely. You can add information using one or more subordinating clauses, as the example opposite shows.

Beware: if you overload a sentence with too much information, spread over a number of subordinating clauses, you could lose your reader's attention.

Main clause

Relative clause

The house, which I had never visited before, seemed strangely familiar.

Notice how the clauses have been separated with commas.

The long and the short

Short punchy sentences can be particularly effective: they add impact to an argument, and surprise or tension to a description. Look at the contrast opposite.

Short sentences are particularly effective when they follow a longer sentence.

Long sentence to contrast with a short sentence to surprise.

Some people believe in leaping out of bed as the sun is rising and settling down to an hour's revision before breakfast, then a couple of hours' more revision before a short jog to revive the brain and another couple of hours' revision before lunchtime. I do not.

In order of importance

You can structure your sentences for emphasis. Important information is usually placed at the end of a sentence.

Arrange your sentences so that the point you want to emphasise comes at the end.

- This sentence gives more emphasis to the revision than the exams because it comes at the end of the sentence:

The final insult is that the dreaded exams come after all that revision.

- This sentence emphasises the dreaded exams, giving the sentence more impact:

The final insult is that after all that revision come the dreaded exams.

Now try this

Write **one** or **two** paragraphs in response to this exam-style question:

6 'Sport and life are quite similar. In both of them, the only thing that matters is winning.'

Write an article arguing **either** *for* **or** *against* this point of view. *(24 marks)*

Aim to include examples of:

- a long sentence followed by a short sentence
- a sentence structured to leave the important information until last.

Putting it into practice

Look at the exam-style question below and read the two sample student answers.

Worked example

6 Many people believe that it is important to follow fashion and look good.

Write an article for a teenage website which argues *for* **or** *against* this idea. *(24 marks)*

Sentence variety

In both writing tasks you should:

- ✓ use a range of sentence structures
- ✓ start your sentences in different ways
- ✓ structure your sentences for effect.

Sample answer

Fashion is important because people judge you on how you look, even though you shouldn't it's difficult not to. Fashion can also be fun because shopping and choosing clothes and seeing what your friends are wearing is really enjoyable. Fashion is also something to talk about and do with your friends because if all your friends are in fashion and like the same fashion then you can swap clothes and tell them how they look.

Notice that:

- each sentence starts in the same way
- each sentence follows the same structure
- sentences are all long and complex, using multiple clauses.

To improve your answer you should add variety.

✗ Vocabulary is frequently repeated.

✗ A limited range of connectives creates repetitive vocabulary and sentence structure.

Improved sample answer

We all judge a book by its cover. We don't mean to but we do. But should we? Even if we don't want to judge others, we expect others to judge us. We primp, preen and polish ourselves for hours, preparing ourselves to be seen by the world. How disappointing would it be if, after all that effort, no one bothered to look and make the right judgement? The truth is that, no matter how much we might not want appearances to matter, they do. They matter very much.

Notice how this answer starts with:

- two short sentences to create an emphatic opening
- a rhetorical question engages reader
- a neatly structured sentence.

The improvement is reflected in the grade.

✓ A second rhetorical question further engages reader.

✓ Long sentence, followed by powerful short sentence further emphasized with repetition.

Now try this

Write the **first two** paragraphs of your answer to the exam-style question above.

Remember to:

- use a range of sentence types and lengths
- start sentences in a variety of ways
- structure sentences for effect.

Had a look ☐ Nearly there ☐ Nailed it! ☐

Full stops, question marks and exclamation marks

Failing to use **full stops, question marks, exclamation marks** and **capital letters** correctly can seriously affect the quality of your writing.

Check your full stops

Most students know that a sentence should start with a capital letter and end with a full stop. However, some students do not always remember to check their punctuation. No matter how strong the rest of your writing skills are, poor punctuation – and full stops in particular – will lose you valuable marks. The most common error is using a comma to join two sentences instead of a full stop to separate them. This is called a **comma splice.**

The comma splice

When you want to tell the reader two pieces of information you can do two things.

✓ Separate them with a full stop:

> Puppies are small and cuddly. People do not seem to realise that they will soon grow.

✓ Join them with a connective:

> Puppies are small and cuddly **but** people do not seem to realise that they will soon grow.

✗ You **cannot** join them with a comma:

> Puppies are small and cuddly, people do not seem to realise that they will soon grow.

Question marks

Always check you have put a question mark at the end of a question – especially a rhetorical question.

Exclamation marks

Be **very** careful in your use of exclamation marks. Follow these golden rules.

- Only use an exclamation mark for an exclamation, e.g. 'Thank goodness!' he cried.
- Use them very sparingly. Don't scatter them randomly throughout your writing, and never put one at the end of a title.
- Never use two or more exclamation marks in a row.

Now try this

Rewrite this student's answer, removing all the comma splices. Try to do this in three different ways by:

- adding connectives
- restructuring some of the sentences
- replacing the comma splices with full stops.

Remember that you do not use a comma to join two pieces of information in a sentence. Use a full stop to separate them, or a connective to join them.

> Puppies are small and cuddly, people do not seem to realise they will soon grow, after a year or more they are puppies no longer, they have grown into huge dogs needing vast amounts of exercise, vast amounts of food and vast amounts of attention. All too often the result is disaster, it's not just furniture that gets chewed and destroyed, worst of all people can be hurt by dogs that have become aggressive through lack of training or lack of care. Before you buy a puppy, make sure you have spent some time with an adult of the same breed, it could save you a lot of time, trouble and heartache.

Commas

It is very important that you feel confident using commas accurately, as the clarity of your complex sentences and lists is dependent on our use of commas. For more on complex sentences, see pages 36 and 80.

Commas and subordinating clauses

In a complex sentence, the main clause and the subordinating clause can usually be swapped around without changing the meaning of the sentence:

I meet new people wherever I go.

- I meet new people – main clause
- wherever I go. – subordinating clause

If you begin a complex sentence with the main clause, there is no need for a comma to separate the clauses.

Wherever I go, I meet new people.

- Wherever I go, – subordinating clause
- I meet new people. – main clause

If you begin a complex sentence with the subordinating clause, use a comma to separate it from the main clause.

Commas and relative clauses

You can add a relative clause to a sentence, giving additional information linked with one of these relative pronouns:

- that
- whose
- where
- who
- which
- when

You should always separate the relative clause from the main clause with commas.

Main clause   Relative clause

The house, which I had never visited before, seemed strangely familiar.

Notice how the clauses have been separated with commas.

Commas in a list

If you are writing a list, add a comma after each word or phrase – apart from the words or phrases which are linked using and.

- Use commas in lists of adjectives:

He was tall, smartly dressed and elegant.

Comma here to separate two items in a list.

No comma here because they are linked with and.

- Use commas in lists of phrases:

There was mud on the floor, mud on the walls, mud on the windows and mud on the ceiling.

Now try this

Look at this exam-style question:

6 'Your school days are the happiest days of your life.' Write an article arguing **either** *for* **or** *against* this point of view. *(24 marks)*

Write **three** to **five** sentences, using commas correctly to separate:

- items in a list
- a main and subordinating clause
- a main and relative clause.

Had a look ☐ Nearly there ☐ Nailed it! ☐

Apostrophes and speech punctuation

Missing or incorrect **apostrophes** and **speech punctuation** are common errors. Make sure you know how to avoid making mistakes with them.

Apostrophes in contractions

When two words are shortened or abbreviated, some letters are missed out or omitted. You should use an apostrophe to show where these letters are missing:

cannot → **can't**
do not → **don't**
I will → **I'll**
let us → **let's**

Abbreviations such as **don't** and **can't** are more informal than the full, unabbreviated versions. Think about your audience when deciding which to use.

Apostrophes of possession

Apostrophes can be used to show that something or someone belongs to someone or something else.

- The boy's hands …
- Betty's sister …
- The dog's collar …
- The school's head teacher …

Note that if the word to which you are adding the apostrophe ends in s you can just add the apostrophe after the s:

The teachers' voices

Mrs Roberts' book

Note that this is a plural: there is more than one teacher.

You can also, when a name ends in s, add an apostrophe and another s:

Mrs Roberts's book

Speech punctuation

- Use speech marks to enclose the words that are spoken.
- Start the speech with a capital letter.
- There is **always** a punctuation mark just before the closing speech marks.
- Use a comma if you are adding who is speaking …
- … followed by a lower case letter immediately after the closing speech marks.
- Use a full stop if you are not adding who is speaking.

'Mum, can I have some sweets?' begged Aran.

'It's nearly dinner time,' his mother replied.

'Mum, I want some sweets.'

'I've just told you,' said his mother patiently.

Now try this

There are **13** punctuation errors in this student's writing. Copy and correct it.

'theres nothing I can do said Garys dad.
'are you sure,' Replied Gary.
'idont know what you mean.' Said his dad.
'i think you do'

Colons, semi-colons, dashes, brackets and ellipses

Using punctuation like **colons**, **semi-colons**, **dashes**, **brackets** and **ellipses** helps you develop your ideas and express yourself clearly.

Semi-colons

You can use semi-colons to link two connected ideas instead of using a connective.

For example, you could write:

> The value of education is enormous and it should be treasured.

Or you could write:

> The value of education is enormous; it should be treasured.

Colons

Use a colon to:

- introduce an example

> Students have two choices: work hard or fail.

- introduce a list

> You will need: a pen, a pencil, a ruler, and an eraser.

- introduce an explanation

> English is my favourite subject: I love learning about punctuation.

Dashes and brackets

These can be used to add extra, but not entirely necessary, information to a sentence.

Before using brackets or dashes, ask yourself: Is this important information? Or would my writing be better without it?

- Dashes can be used in pairs to add information in mid-sentence:

> Several years earlier – though I can't remember when exactly – my grandmother had moved to a remote island off the coast of Scotland.

- Dashes can also be used singularly at the end of a sentence, to suggest a pause before an afterthought:

> I'm sure there was a reason – but no one ever told me what it was.

- Brackets must be used in **pairs**:

> The house (which my mother hated and my father loved) was about a mile from the sea.

Ellipses

- You can use an ellipsis in dialogue to suggest a dramatic pause or to show someone falling into silence:

> 'I don't know where I …' He looked mystified.

> 'And the winner is …'

- Using an ellipsis to suggest tension in descriptive writing can seem clichéd. Rely instead on your choice of language and sentence structure to create tension:

✗

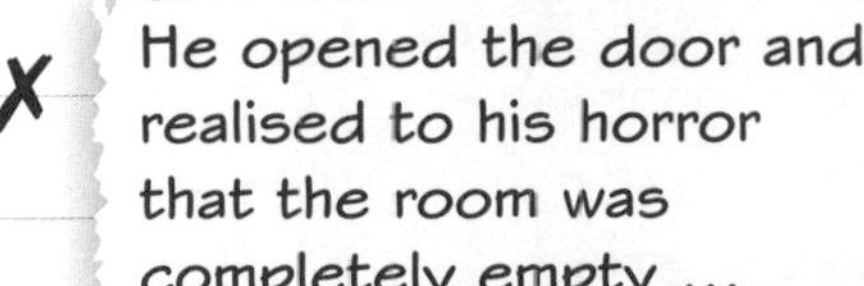
He opened the door and realised to his horror that the room was completely empty …

✓

> He opened the door. The room was completely empty.

Had a look ☐ Nearly there ☐ Nailed it! ☐

Putting it into practice

Look at the exam-style question below and read the two sample student answers.

Worked example

5 Your school or college magazine is publishing a series of articles with the title, 'I couldn't live without …' Write your article, informing the reader about the one thing that you couldn't live without and explaining why it is so important to you. It could be an object, a hobby or interest, a person, or even an idea. *(16 marks)*

Punctuation

In both writing tasks you should:

- ✓ punctuate accurately
- ✓ use a range of punctuation.

Sample answer

I could'nt live without football, its something I've always loved. I love playing it and watching it whether its a few friends having a kickabout at lunchtime or an FA Cup final on the telly. There are lots of reasons it means so much to me. One is that my dad loves football so its something we have in common. He does'nt play football but we can spend hours talking about it, who scored, who didnt score who should be playing and who should be dropped.

✗ Incorrectly placed apostrophes.

✗ Comma splice. This should either be a semi-colon or a full stop followed by a new sentence.

✗ Missing apostrophe.

✗ Missed opportunity for a colon to introduce a list.

✗ Missing comma separating items in a list.

Note that the use of full stops in the first answer is **generally** accurate.

Improved sample answer

The only thing which I cannot imagine ever being without is my dog. She doesn't bark, she doesn't growl, she doesn't jump up; she's perfect in every way. Just the sight of her floppy ears, her wagging tail and her shiny black eyes can put a smile on my face. I remember when I got her: it was my ninth birthday, a day I will always remember. I opened all my presents – none of which I can remember now – and my mum said she had one more surprise for me. She brought in a small cardboard box.

The full stops in the improved answer are **completely** accurate.

✓ Correct use of apostrophe.

✓ Commas, semi-colons and colons are all used accurately. Notice how the commas separate items in a list, the colon is used to introduce an explanation, and the semi-colon acts like a full stop.

Dashes like these are used to add additional information.

Now try this

Write the first paragraph of your answer to the above exam-style question. Aim to use a range of punctuation accurately, including commas, apostrophes, colons and semi colons.

Always remember to check your punctuation – especially full stops – for accuracy.

Common spelling errors 1

There are some spelling mistakes that occur again and again in students' exam responses. You should learn how to avoid making them.

Would have, could have, should have

Students often use **would of** or **should of** or **could of** when they should use **would have**, **should have**, or **could have**. For example:

✗ Global warming could of been prevented. We should of started thinking more carefully about the environment long ago.

This is what should have been written:
could **have** ✓ should **have** ✓

Our, are

Students often confuse our and are:

- **our** means **belonging to us**
- **are** is from the verb **to be**.

✗ We should always look after are bodies. They our precious.

This is what should have been written:
our bodies ✓ **are** precious ✓

There, their, they're

Make sure you learn these spellings:

- **their** means belonging to **them**
- **there** is used to describe the position of something (**It's over there**) and in the phrases **There is** or **There are**
- **they're** is an abbreviation of **they are**.

✗ Their were three people at the table, all eating there dinner.

✓ ~~Their~~ There were three people at the table, all eating ~~there~~ their dinner.

Affect, effect

One of these is a verb, and the other a noun:
affect is a verb
effect is usually used as a noun.
So, for example, you may have been **affected** by a problem. But the problem had an **effect** on you. If the word has got **an** or **the** in front of it, it's a noun, so it's spelt **effect**.

Remember: don't be afraid to use an effective word because you're not sure about the spelling.

ly or -ley?

When you add -ly to a word, make sure you don't swap the 'l' and the 'e':

definite + ly = definitely

bravley ✗ bravely ✓
safley ✗ safely ✓
rudley ✗ rudely ✓

There are **very few** words which end in -ley. Learn these examples: alley, medley, trolley, valley.

Its or it's?

It's is an abbreviation of **it is**. **Its** means belonging to **it**.

✗ Its the end of it's life.

✓ ~~Its~~ It's the end of ~~it's~~ its life.

Now try this

Look back at the last five pieces of writing you have completed. Have you made any of these common spelling errors? If so, correct them.

Common spelling errors 2

Spend some time studying common spelling mistakes so that you don't make them in your exam.

Your and you're

Learn the difference between these two words:

- **your** means **belonging to you**
- **you're** is an abbreviation of **you are.**

✗ Your having the time of you're life.

✓ ~~Your~~ You're having the time of ~~you're~~ your life.

Remember: **A lot** is two words. **Alot of people love chocolate** is wrong, but **A lot of people love chocolate** is correct.

We're, wear, were and where

Make sure you are familiar with each of these:

- **we're** is an abbreviation of **we are**
- **wear** is a verb referring to clothing – e.g. **What are you wearing tonight?**
- **were** is the past tense of are – e.g. **they are,** they were
- **where** is a question word referring to place – e.g. **Where are we going?**

✗ Wear we're you? Were leaving now.

✓ ~~Wear we're~~ Where were you? ~~Were~~ We're leaving now.

Two, too, to

Getting these words wrong is quite a common error:

- **to** indicates place, direction or position – e.g. **I went to Spain.**
- **too** means **also** or an **excessive amount** – e.g. **I went too far.**
- **two** is a number.

✗ It's to difficult to get too the highest level.

✓ It's ~~to~~ too difficult to get ~~too~~ to the highest level.

Of, off

The easiest way to remember the difference is by listening to the sound of the word you want to use:

- **of** is pronounced ov
- **off** rhymes with cough.

✗ He jumped of the top off the wall.

✓ He jumped ~~of~~ off the top ~~off~~ of the wall.

Past, passed

Aim to get these two right:

- **passed** is the past tense of the verb to pass – e.g. **He passed all his GCSEs.**
- **past** refers to time that has gone by, or position – e.g. **That's all in the past; He ran past the school.**

✗ She past out at ten passed six.

✓ She ~~past~~ passed out at ten ~~passed~~ past six.

Who's and whose

Whose is a question word referring to belonging, e.g. **Whose book is this?**

Who's is an abbreviation of **who is.**

✗ Whose wearing who's coat?

✓ ~~Whose~~ Who's wearing ~~who's~~ whose coat?

Now try this

Look back at the last five pieces of writing you have completed. Have you made any of these common spelling errors? If so, correct them.

Common spelling errors 3

Some of the most frequently misspelt are listed below. Make sure you learn how to spell these words properly.

amusement
argument

Notice the 'e' here but not here.

opportunity
disappoint
embarrassing
beginning
occasionally
difficult
disappear
possession
recommend

Check which letters are **doubled** and which are not.

privilege
definitely
separately
conscious
conscience
experience
independence

Look closely at the vowels – 'e', 'i' or 'a'.

business — Silent 'i' in the middle.

believe weird — 'ei' or 'ie'?

rhythm — Two 'h's, but no vowels.

decision — Get the 'c' and the 's' round the right way.

grateful — Not greatful; **grat**eful = to show **grat**itude.

Learning correct spellings

Find a hidden word. Look for words hidden within the word you are learning. For example, **separate** becomes much easier to remember when you notice that there's a rat in the middle of it:

sep **a rat** e

Say what you see. Say the word aloud, breaking it up into syllables and pronouncing them as they are written. For example, read these syllables aloud:

def / in / ite / ly

Now try this

Test yourself on these spellings. Learn any which you get wrong, then you could ask a friend or family member to re-test you.

Proofreading

It is essential that you leave time at the end of the exam to check your work. It could make all the difference.

What kinds of mistakes do you make?

Here's a list of common errors:

- spelling mistakes
- missing or incorrect punctuation
- grammatical errors such as misused, repeated or missing words.

Most people make **all three** kinds of mistakes, especially when they are writing in a hurry.

Ideally, you should check your work through three times:

- once for spelling
- once for punctuation
- once to check it makes clear sense, with no misused, repeated or missing words.

You **will** have made mistakes. Aim to find **five or more** in each of your answers.

Alarm bells

Train your proofreading brain to ring an alarm bell whenever you come across **their, there, its, it's** or any one of the common spelling errors that everyone makes. When the alarm rings, **stop!** Double check that you've used the correct spelling.

How to check your spelling

If you know you've spelt a word incorrectly, but you're not sure of the correct spelling, try it three or four different ways in the margin. Pick the one that looks right:

seperatly	separetly
separately ✓	separatley

Reading your work backwards – from bottom to top, right to left – stops you thinking about the meaning of your writing and makes you focus on spelling.

Checking for sense: tips

1. When you are checking for sense, try to read 'aloud inside your head' imagining you can hear your voice.
2. Remember to leave time to check your work at the end of the exam. If you check each answer as soon as you've finished writing it, you'll see what you **think** you wrote, not what you **actually** wrote.
3. If you come across a sentence which is clumsy, doesn't make sense, or both… cross it out and try expressing it in a different way.

Putting it right

Accurate writing achieves higher marks than neat writing. So, if you find a mistake – whether it's a word, a sentence, or a whole paragraph – **cross it out**. Put **one neat line** through the mistake and add your correction by:

- using one of these / ~~to make a mistake~~ (to guide the reader)
- or by using an asterisk.*

If you forget to start a new paragraph, use // to mark where one paragraph ends and the next one begins.

* To tell the reader to read this bit next.

Now try this

Look over five pieces of writing you have produced recently. How many mistakes can you find?

Putting it into practice

Look at the exam-style question below and read the two sample student answers.

Worked example

6 Your local newspaper recently printed an article which argued: 'Every teenager should have a part-time job. It teaches them the value of money and prepares them for life.' Write a letter to the editor, replying to this article. Argue **either** *for* **or** *against* the writer of the article's point of view. *(24 marks)*

Proofreading

For both your writing tasks you should:

- spend about 3–5 minutes carefully checking your work
- correct any spelling errors
- correct any punctuation errors
- ensure your writing makes clear sense.

Finding and changing errors could really improve your answer.

Sample answer

Everyone says GCSEs have got easyer but they dont realise how difficult they are and how how much work we have to do at school. There just isn't time to do all the school work and have a part-time job, we need some to rest and and enjoy ourselves. On an avarage day I go to school for six hours, get home and do an hour or two of homework. I could go out to work in the evenings but Id get home late and be realy tired at school the next day which would make it realy dificult to concentrate at school the next day.

Make sure you spend some time checking your answers. The second sentence:

- is clumsily written
- has errors
- is not clear in its meaning.

✗ Spelling errors

✗ Punctuation errors

Improved sample answer

Working for my money has certainly taught me its value. For example, when I was younger and wanted to buy something, I had to pester my mum.* Now, because I've e→arned my money, ~~I can buy what I want. Because of that I always make sure I know I want what I'm buying.~~ I make very sure I'm not wasting my money on something I ~~dont~~ →don't really need.

* Usually, once I'd got it, I would realise that I didn't really want it anymore.

✓ Spelling and punctuation errors both corrected.

It's fine to cross out clumsy writing and add in something that is easier to read and understand.

✓ The additional explanation effectively reinforces the argument.

Now try this

Look back at a piece of writing you have completed recently. Check it **three** times, looking for:

- sentences that are clumsily written or unclear
- missing or repeated words
- spelling mistakes
- punctuation errors.

Aim to find at least **five** mistakes and correct them.

Answers

SECTION A: READING

1. Questions 1 and 2

1 Selecting relevant information.
2 Explain effect of presentation.

2. Questions 3 and 4

1 Select and infer relevant information.
2 Skill of inference tested in question 3.
3 Compare effect/effectiveness of language.

3. Planning your exam time

- Q2: 12 minutes.
- Q3: 12 minutes.
- Q4: 24 minutes.

4. Reading the questions

- Source 3, and **either** Source 1 **or** Source 2.
- *compare, ways, language, used, effect*
- Language
- *Give some examples and analyse what the effects are.*
- 16 marks.
- 24 minutes.

5. Approaching the exam paper

1 Q3: 12 minutes. (9.39–9.51 am)
Q4: 24 minutes. (9.51–10.15 am)
2 Q2: *Source 2, explain, headline, picture, effective, link, text.*
Q3: *Source 3, explain, thoughts and feelings, Sally Bland, during, South American expedition.*
Q4: *Source 3 and* ***either*** *Source 1* ***or*** *Source 2, compare, language, effect, examples, analyse, effects.*

6. Skimming for the main idea

For example: School proms have become an opportunity to show off how much money you have got but should be about having a good time.

7. Annotating the sources

Key points could include:
- 'Here': orientates the reader, engaging them in the story
- 'extraordinarily dedicated': adverb for emphasis
- 'They have to be.': short blunt sentence
- '£100 a week': factual information
- 'Training is torture': alliteration
- 'callused and blistered': vivid descriptive language
- 'next to no chance of winning medals': final item in a long list contrasting with their dedication.

8. Selecting information

Key points could include:
- Collins is 'a bit of a mystery'
- she is married to a TV actor
- she doesn't do publicity
- she hasn't even met her UK publishers.

9. Purpose and audience

Key points could include:
- focuses on beauty, comfort and relaxation, appealing to adult audience
- persuasive language: 'great ... true ... live long in the memory'.

10/11. Putting it into practice

Answers should include three further points, as these examples show.
- Achievement is linked to how much homework students do, not how much is set.
- Improvement in achievement is more closely linked to effort than to ability.
- Students who enjoy school achieve better results.
- Schools can improve enjoyment by improving the 'behavioural climate'.
- A good primary school contributes to success in Maths and Science at secondary school.

12. The writer's viewpoint

Key points could include these.
- The writer is concerned at the use of animal testing around the world.
- The list of countries suggests the issue is widespread.
- The list of examples of animal cruelty is to shock the reader.
- Use of dramatic, emotive language, e.g. 'forced ... kill'.

13. Fact, opinion and expert evidence

Fact: James is 13.
Opinion: James was lucky.
Expert evidence: '"They believe there is nothing else out there," says Mr Mitchell.'

14. Inference

Answers could include the following quotations:
- 'breathtaking', 'famous the world over', 'exceptional', 'most challenging', 'ever'
- All suggest the scale and impact of his achievement.

15. Point-Evidence-Explain

1 For example: The writer uses a stream of negative language to describe Britain. For example, he describes Britain as 'sleazy'. This suggests that Britain is rundown, dirty and immoral.
2 Effective sentences should use connecting phrases to link students' P-E-E.

16/17. Putting it into practice

Answers should include at least three points, and could include the following.
- Mills had always wanted to 'do radio'.
- His first on-air experience was doing the chart rundown.
- He is a loyal friend: he's still in contact with his friend Lee.
- He was hugely disappointed when told to leave.
- He comes from humble beginnings: a small town in Hampshire.

- He followed his dream and achieved it through volunteering.

18. Identifying presentational devices 1

Answers could include:
- dominant colour orange suggests sunny, positive attitude to success
- information/advice summarised in bold headings, some more positive and appealing, e.g. 'Pamper yourself'
- image reflects target audience; hat and sunglasses suggest this information is relevant even to 'cool' teenagers!

19. Identifying presentational devices 2

Answers could include: at least three presentational and structural features, e.g. sections, boxes, bullet points, numbered or lettered lists, tables, paragraphs.

20. Using P-E-E to comment on presentational devices

Key points could include:
- subheading adds information to further engage the reader and highlights writer's viewpoint
- image illustrates the article; smiling children suggests they are enjoying competition; winning tape suggests emphasis on winning/competition.

21. Commenting on headlines

Key points could include the following:
Headline:
- summarises story; alliteration adds impact/drama; emotive language ('batters').

Subheading:
- adds further information; use of facts; emotive language 'homeless… torrential… strike').

22. Image and effect

Answers should describe what the photo will show and what the weather is like.

23. Linking comments on presentation to the text

Answers should explain how the headline, subheading and photo are effective and how they link with the text. They may include some of the points from the Source 1 annotations.

24. Selecting evidence

Answer to be structured using P-E-E and may include some of the points from the sample answer on page 24.

25. Embedding quotations

For example: The writer fills the article with positive language, suggesting that athletes can 'inspire' young people, giving them 'self-respect' and making them more 'healthy' and 'motivated'. This range of language suggests that sporting role models can have an enormously and entirely positive impact on young people in many different ways.

26/27. Putting it into practice

Key points could include the following.
Subheading:
- develops the idea of secrecy and of revelation ('what life is really like')
- suggests humble beginnings ('council estate') compared to success ('a long career in the Premier League')
- suggests ambition ('all he wanted') compared to disillusionment ('question everything').

Image:
- shadow covering face like a mask emphasises anonymity and secrecy.

28. Develop your explanations

For example:
- 'I leap.': Short sentence at end of a paragraph creates blunt, dramatic cliffhanger; 'leap' has connotations of energy and recklessness
- 'an instant explosion of pain and noise and white': Pattern of three and lack of description suggest an overwhelming but indescribable experience as though Grylls can only recount a very basic, instinctive response; explosion suggests danger, violence and extreme force.

29. Word classes

- Descriptive list, richly filled with adjectives creates a vivid visual image.
- Present participles (*-ing* words) of action verbs create a strong sense of movement and noise.

30/31. Putting it into practice

Answers could include these.
- The only description of human contact during or after the crash is when the wrier 'locked eyes' with another passenger, suggesting a feeling of solitary fear and isolation.
- Description of the 'incredible force' of the impact leaving the writer 'amazed' that she 'walked away without any injuries'
- Vivid description of waiting to be rescued: 'soaking', 'shivering', 'wind howling' for ten minutes though it 'felt like an hour' suggests feelings of pain and fear.
- The crash does not seem to have had a lasting effect: the writer was keen to fly again, even though it felt 'a little unnerving'.

32. Connotations

1/2 'lowing herd' suggests a group of noisy animals, implying that they do not think or express themselves intelligently as individuals.
'targeting' suggests a finely focused aim, perhaps even presenting the targeted viewers as victims of an attack.

33. Rhetorical devices 1

Alliteration for emphasis: 'a hub for half the globe', 'fluctuating fortunes'.
Repetition for emphasis: '**any**thing you could not buy there or **any**one'.
Repetition to link ideas: 'if **you have not** been there, **you have not** really seen the world'.
Pattern of three suggests range and variety: 'drugs, late-night noise and multi-culturalism run riot', 'refuge, or fame, or fortune'.

34. Rhetorical devices 2

Answers could include these.
- emotive language/hyperbole to exaggerate the point: 'obsessed'
- alliteration for emphasis: 'fear of failure'
- contrast to highlight difference of 'my generation' and 'our children' and 'Chinese and Indian children'
- pattern of three/repetition to emphasise ambition: 'to earn money, to have good careers, to make something of our lives'.

35. Figurative language

Simile: 'like vast uncut diamonds' suggests size and value.
Metaphor: 'a floating white blanket of ice' suggests it completely covers the sea.

36. Identifying sentence types

1 Complex – longer sentence with one part dependent on the other.
2 Compound – contains two or more verbs.
3 Simple – gives on piece of information.
4 Complex – longer sentence with on part dependent on the other.
5 Compound – simple sentences joined by 'and'.
6 Minor – does not contain a verb.

37. Commenting on sentence types

Answers should focus on sentence length and/or structure, commenting on the reasons for the writer's choice, e.g. audience, mood, emphasis, impact, etc.

38/39. Putting it into practice

Points could include these.
- Simile: 'People are like rivers.' An intriguing visual image, explained in the subsequent sentence.
- Series of short simple sentences: 'He worked, aged 12 to 14, in a bakery. From 14 he took the only road open to him. He went into the pit and stayed there. Escape was impossible.' A blunt sequence of short, simple and compound sentences, suggesting inevitability of this course of events.
- 'dragged' suggests hard physical effort, and reluctance.
- Alliteration/metaphor: 'the reluctance and resentment of a refugee' emphasises displacement and discomfort.
- List: 'Goal magazine ... football stickers ... Newcastle shirt' emphasises football as the only shared interest of father and son.
- Simile: 'as dark as a cave' suggests unwelcoming, daunting.
- Simile: 'fingers as thin as splinters' suggests danger/pain.
- Pattern of three: 'his reticence, his detachment and his apparent lack of tenderness' emphasises extent of father's emotional distance from son.
- Pattern of three: 'football doesn't matter; or that football is just a game'; or even 'Well, it's only football." emphasises range of negative attitudes to football.
- Short sentences: 'No, it isn't. Not for me.' An emphatic negation of these attitudes.
- Contrast: 'Without football, we were strangers under a shared roof. With it, we were father and son.' Emphasises the difference that football made to their lives.

40. Making the best comments

For example:
Evidence: 'my brain – not the size of my bust – was my ultimate weapon.'
Comments on:
- viewpoint – intelligence is far more important than appearance
- purpose – the writer belittles appearance to convince the reader of the importance of intelligence
- language choice – the alliteration of 'brain' and 'bust' encourages the reader to link and compare their relative value.
- sentence structure – the phrase 'not the size of my bust' is separated from the rest of the sentence with dashes, adding emphasis to the writer's dismissal of its importance.
- effect on the reader – the belittling phrase 'the size of my bust' creates a humorous tone to engage the reader further.

41. Comment on language and purpose: argue and persuade

Answers to include: rhetorical questions, hyperbole, emotive language, contrast, lists, repetition – and their effect.

42. Comment on language and purpose: describe

Answers to include: language choice, the five senses, figurative language – and their effect.

43. Comment on language and purpose: inform and explain

Answers should include: structure, tone, facts and statistics – and their effect.

44/45. Putting it into practice

Points could include these.
- 'Skim a stone, run around in the rain, play conkers, make a mud pie.' Alliteration contributes to the appeal of these activities.
- 'free range' suggests positive, healthy, etc.
- 'tiny mishaps': hyperbole underplays the danger and damage of a long list of activities and their consequences.
- 'The outdoors is a treasure trove': metaphor suggests wealth, variety and worth.
- Surprising contrast of 'no material riches' with 'privileged' emphasises the worth of such outdoor activities.

46. Looking closely at language

Answers could include these.
Engaging the reader:
- 'sizzle so seductively' onomatopoeia creates an aural as well as visual image to engage the reader's senses.

Use of contrast:
- contrast of 'high quality, dry cured bacon' with meat 'pumped with water…'

47. Planning to compare language

Here are some examples.

1 *Both texts use language to engage the reader from the start.* Source 1 uses a short exclamation, with the alliterative 'fun-filled' to emphasise the reader's potential enjoyment. Source 2 lists a range of scams in a pattern of three to introduce the topic and invite the reader's recognition as we have all experienced one or more of these.
2 *Both texts use emotive language for different purposes.* Source 1 uses the word 'murderer' to suggest the dramatic and exciting onboard adventure to persuade the reader to book, while Source 2 describes the elderly being 'duped' because their 'brain has deteriorated or is damaged' to prompt the reader's sympathy.
3 *Both texts use language choice to achieve their purpose.* Source 1 persuades through its use of positive language such as 'tranquil' and 'delicious', suggesting both relaxation and luxury are available in addition to the exciting murder mystery activity. Source 2 uses facts to inform the reader, using the highly specialised scientific language 'ventromedial prefrontal cortex' to suggest the information is valid and reliable.

48. Comparing language

1 For example, short sentences, hyperbole (six postcodes, mass upheaval), informal language.
2 Effective answers should compare the use of language and its effects.

49. Answering a compare question

Answers should focus on a range of language techniques and their effects and may use sentence starters and structure suggested on the page.

50/51. Putting it into practice

Points could include these.
Source 1:
- direct address engages and involves the reader: '**our** education system'
- emotive language to highlight the issue: 'horribly wrong', 'soared'
- persuasive use of statistics: 'a rise of almost 13%'
- alliterative/metaphorical description: 'a steely determination to succeed' emphasising the power and strength of determination above academic qualifications
- contrast of 'training' versus 'education' to emphasise the difference
- short emphatic simple sentence to drive home the argument: 'Let's give young people the courage and ambition to go for it.'

Source 2:
- direct address to engage and persuade the reader to enter the competition: 'go galactic ... get cracking!'
- alliteration creates an engaging heading: 'cracking ... competition'
- list suggests variety of interests: 'rocket launching science, lunar landscape art, deep space design or galactic gizmo technology'
- list suggests variety of different approaches to persuade the reader to enter: 'make models, take photographs, draw plans'.

SECTION B: WRITING

52. Reading the questions

- A national newspaper audience of adults/older teenagers.
- Describe, explain.
- Article.
- The perfect school.

53. The questions and planning your exam time

- students, parents, teachers
- argue, persuade
- magazine article, website article
- television is a waste of time, money isn't everything, tourist information

54. Writing for an audience

For example: You may think you've got ages to prepare for your GCSEs. You may think you don't need to worry about them just yet. But time flies and it won't be long before you're sitting in that exam hall. So it's important to start getting ready for them now.
(Note the use of some informal features, e.g. abbreviations such as 'you've', which are appropriate to this audience but would not be in a more formal text.)

55. Writing for a purpose: inform and explain

1 Subheadings could include:
   - schoolwork
   - talking to your teenager
   - what to do when friends come round
   - hair and clothes
   - bedtime.
2 Tone: an informal tone suggesting a friendly and supportive voice, but using standard English to suggest the information is reliable and trustworthy.
3 Facts and statistics: e.g. research suggests teenagers need more sleep, suffer from mood swings caused by hormonal changes, etc.

56. Writing for a purpose: describe

For example: The dark closed around me as the door clicked shut. I rattled the handle and, as I realised it was locked, a shudder climbed up my spine.
(Note the use of the senses (*dark, clicked, rattled*); the physical symptoms of fear (*shudder*); and the use of personification (*climbed*)).

57. Writing for purpose: argue and persuade

Points + evidence examples:
- could be the beginning of a great career; many international superstars such as Lady Gaga first performed in school talent shows
- could win you some money; the top three acts win cash prizes
- all proceeds go to a great cause; if everyone bought a ticket we could buy a herd of goats for a village in a developing country.

Counter argument examples:
You might think standing on stage will be embarrassing, but if you perform in a group, you can support each other.

Rhetorical device examples:
- Fame, fortune and a fantastic future could be just around the corner. (alliteration/pattern of three)
- What's the worst that can happen? (rhetorical question)
- One minute you're standing on stage, the next you're on top of the world. (metaphor/hyperbole)

58. Putting it into practice

Answers should include:
- audience: the head of school/college
- form: letter
- purpose: argue for or against
- topic: sell playing fields, build science block and library

59. Form: letters and emails

Key features: address in top right hand corner with date underneath; name and address of person writing to left hand side; Yours sincerely or Yours faithfully; name underneath signature.

60. Form: articles

Make sure a key idea is in paragraph 1, more detail in paragraph 2 and a quotation in paragraph 3.

61. Form: information sheets

Make sure there is a heading, some key subheadings and some structural features.

62. Putting it into practice

Key points:
- Language should be formal standard English.
- Opening paragraph could sum up the reason for writing and outline of your argument.
- Conclusion could sum up your argument and explain why you feel it is so important, e.g. what would be the consequences of young people volunteering or not volunteering?

63. Planning an answer: describe

Plans should include four or five key ideas and a range of supporting details/language ideas.

64. Planning an answer: inform or explain

A possible structure:
- Paragraph 1: introduction: describe/explain the 'one thing'.
- Paragraph 2: explain how/when you realised it was so important.
- Paragraph 3: explain how it could make a difference to teenage life.
- Paragraph 4: explain how it could make a difference throughout people's entire lives.

65. Planning an answer: argue or persuade

A possible plan:
- Introduction – hundreds of channels, 24 hours a day, television can dominate
- Point 1 – TV can be informative/educational.
- Point 2 – shared experience of high quality drama, etc. (no different to theatre but cheaper and more accessible)
- Counter argument: some say it takes over our lives; they need to learn how to turn it off.
- Conclusion: like anything, TV is good and bad; it depends on how it's used. Used carefully/selectively it can bring people together, entertain, inform and educate.

66. Beginnings

1 For example:
   - Do we ever question the purpose of school? Or do we just go there every day because we have to?
   - Exam results can affect our future, but the experience of school can change our lives forever.
   - Nearly half of 16-year-olds in the UK do not achieve five good passes at GCSE.

2 **Exam results can affect our future, but the experience of school can change our lives forever.** While Year 11 students are constantly subjected to their teachers panicking about looming exams, we should remember how relatively unimportant those exams really are. School does not just teach us enough maths and geography to get a GCSE or two. School helps teach us how to live in the world.
(**Note that the bold opening sentence is developed and justified** in the remainder of the paragraph as the writer's argument is introduced and outlined: exams are unimportant; school teaches us much more than how to pass them.)

67. Endings

For example: It is important to work hard at school, to achieve the best results we can for our own satisfaction - but the lessons we learn about being with other people, about setting goals and working towards them, about cooperation and survival will stay with us forever. School days may not be the happiest days of our lives; but they can teach us how to be healthy and happy with ourselves and each other for the rest of our lives. And isn't that more important than a handful of A*s?
(**Note** the first sentence of this conclusion summarises the writer's argument; the second adds a positive note; the final sentence asks a rhetorical question, further promoting their argument.)

68. Putting it into practice

Effective plans will include:
- ideas for an introduction and conclusion
- a range of key points
- some developed detail for each key point
- key points logically sequenced.

69. Paragraphing

If students choose to add a paragraph to the first example they should use Point-Evidence-Explain.
If they have added a paragraph to the second example they need to have clearly introduced the reader to the content of the paragraph then developed it and added detail.

70. Using connectives

For example:
- Revision is essential preparation for exams **therefore/ consequently** it is important to plan time for it.
- **Moreover/In addition**, revision can build your confidence.
- **For example**, in a subject **such as** English, confident writers can often produce more effective responses.

- **In particular**, this is true of argument writing **because** the writer must feel sure of their ideas and convey this certainty to the reader.
- **In the same way**, the reader's response will be all the stronger when guided by a confident descriptive writer.
- **However**, the writer's confidence must be based on skill and understanding achieved through careful revision. Self-belief is not enough.

71. Putting it into practice

Effective answers will:
- be structured using Point-Evidence-Explain
- sequence and signal their argument using a range of connectives.

72. Getting the right tone

For example: Celebrities have an extraordinary amount of power and influence in our society. Some time ago, a famous singer was due to open a shop in our local area. A friend of mine could not contain her excitement. To her it was the most important event of her life. This is surely a worrying symptom of an unhealthy obsession with celebrity.

73. Synonyms

For example: The idea of celebrities as perfect role models is not the only misguided ~~idea~~ concept connected with the world of the ~~celebrity~~ famous. Some people have the ~~idea~~ notion that ~~celebrities~~ superstars should be consulted on everything from international politics to haircare.

74. Choosing vocabulary for effect: describe

For example: A bead of sweat trickled down my forehead and ran into my eye. My eyelid flickered, twitching anxiously as it blinked away the pain. I could feel my shirt stuck to the sweat pooling on my back and the tremor in my stomach becoming a violent jolting. It was getting closer. (**Note** how this response focuses closely on the physical symptoms of the feeling of fear, but does not yet reveal the cause of it, hoping to intrigue the reader.)

75. Choosing vocabulary for effect: argue and persuade

For example: In the UK at this very moment hundreds of children, some as young as five, are being kept in appalling conditions. They are caged for up to seven hours a day. They are often made to sit in silence while aggressive adults hurl abuse at them. They are subjected to a ruthless regime of punishments. Most shockingly of all, this brutal and barbaric treatment is accepted as normal despite the suffering it causes.
Note:
- the use of negative emotive language (appalling, ruthless, etc.) to emphasise the paragraph's central idea
- language chosen for its connotations of imprisonment and torture (caged, brutal, barbaric).

76. Language for effect 1

For example:
- rhetorical question – Do you want to live a long and healthy life?
- contrast – Roaming the great outdoors and breathing lungfuls of fresh air in the sunshine is much more enjoyable than sitting in a stale, airless room staring mindlessly at the television
- list – Obesity can increase your risk of diabetes, heart attack, depression, arthritis, liver failure, and breathing difficulties
- repetition – Exercise can improve your health. Exercise can improve your happiness. Exercise can change your life.

77. Language for effect 2

For example:
- direct address – You would never believe the pressure my mum inflicted on me
- pattern of three – She nagged, pestered and hounded me for days
- hyperbole – I thought my head was going to explode
- alliteration – This was going to be the most miserable minute of my entire life.

78. Language for effect 3

For example:
- simile – For many young people, childhood is **like a race** which should be won as soon as possible
- metaphor – Childhood **is a rare and precious jewel** which we should treasure
- personification – This relentless pressure **batters children** and their childhood into the ground.

79. Putting it into practice

Effective answers should include:
- a range of well chosen and varied vocabulary
- simile, metaphor and personification used **appropriately** and **sparingly**
- a range of language techniques for effect, e.g. repetition, alliteration, etc.

80. Sentence variety 1

For example:
- simple – My bedroom is tiny.
- compound – I can just about stand up and raise my arms without touching the walls on either side.
- complex + subordinating clause – If it ever got cleaned, I would have a lovely view of my neighbour's bathroom window
- complex + relative clause – The window, which is about the size of a postage stamp, is filthy
- minor – Lovely.

81. Sentence variety 2

For example:
- pronoun – I was waiting alone in a classroom.
- article – An eerie silence had fallen.
- preposition – Beyond the classroom door, I heard footsteps.
- *-ing* word – Holding my breath, I waited.
- adjective – Empty and cold, the classroom did nothing to comfort me.
- adverb – Slowly I realised there was a man standing in the doorway.
- connective – Although I had never seen him before, I knew immediately why he was there.

82. Sentences for effect

For example:

- Life, many people say, is a game for winners and, if you are not a winner, you are a loser who has not worked hard enough or focused clearly enough on your goals. They could not be more wrong.
(**Note** that the first sentence has been intentionally extended using multiple clauses.)
- Whether I'm playing Monopoly, taking a test or running the hundred metres, I always come last.
(**Note** how the key information is placed in the final clause.)

83. Putting it into practice

Effective answers should:

- use a range of simple, compound, complex and minor sentences
- use a range of sentence lengths
- start sentences in a variety of ways
- feature sentences structured for effect.

84. Full stops, question marks and exclamation marks

For example:
Puppies are small and cuddly, **however** people do not seem to realise they will soon grow**.** **A**fter a year or more they are puppies no longer**.** They have grown into huge dogs needing vast amounts of exercise, vast amounts of food and vast amounts of attention. All too often the result is disaster – **and** it's not just furniture that gets chewed and destroyed. **W**orst of all people can be hurt by dogs that have become aggressive through lack of training or lack of care. Before you buy a puppy, make sure you have spent some time with an adult of the same breed. **It** could save you a lot of time, trouble and heartache.

85. Commas

For example:

- a list – Nursery school, primary school, middle school and secondary school make up a large proportion of our early lives.
- Main + subordinating clause – Although there may be difficult moments, the friendships we make at school can last a lifetime.
- Main + relative clause – Those difficult moments, which seem terrible at the time, are easily outnumbered by the happy ones.

86. Apostrophes and speech punctuation

The corrections are shown in bold.
'There**'**s nothing I can do**,'** said Gary**'**s dad.
'Are you sure**?'** replied Gary.
'I don't know what you mean**,'** said his dad.
'I think you do.**'**

88. Putting it into practice

Effective answers should include a range of accurate punctuation including commas, apostrophes, colons and semi-colons.

89. Common spelling errors 1

Are students spotting all their spelling mistakes?

90. Common spelling errors 2

Are students spotting all their spelling mistakes?

91. Common spelling errors 3

Are students using effective strategies to learn words?

92. Proofreading

Are students spotting errors in their writing?

93. Putting it into practice

Effective answers should contain at least five corrected mistakes.

There are no questions printed on this page.

There are no questions printed on this page.

There are no questions printed on this page.

There are no questions printed on this page.

There are no questions printed on this page.

There are no questions printed on this page.

There are no questions printed on this page.

There are no questions printed on this page.